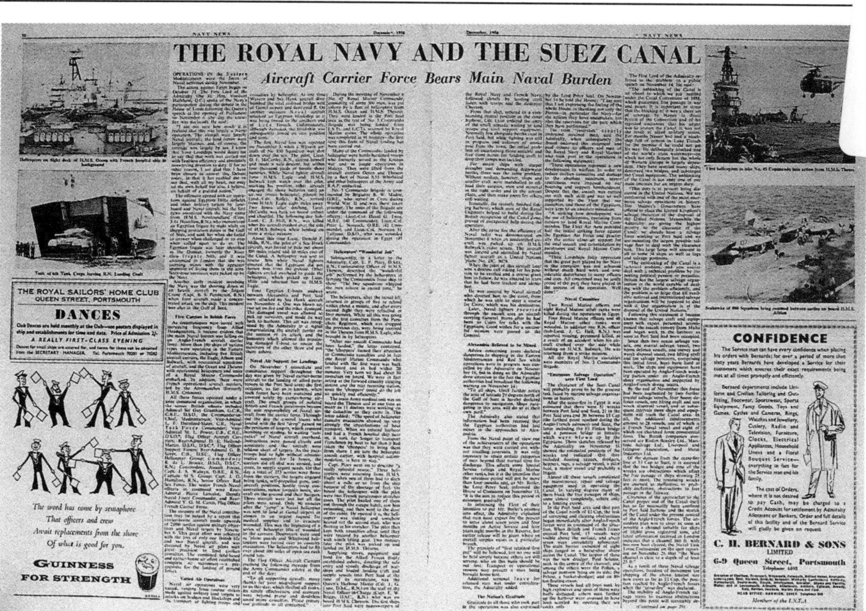

NAVY NEWS

THE ROYAL NAVY AND THE SUEZ CANAL

Aircraft Carrier Force Bears Main Naval Burden

THE ROYAL SAILORS' HOME CLUB
QUEEN STREET, PORTSMOUTH

DANCES

A REALLY FIRST-CLASS EVENING

The word has come by semaphore
That officers and crew
Await replacements from the shore
Of what is good for you.

GUINNESS FOR STRENGTH

CONFIDENCE

C. H. BERNARD & SONS LIMITED
6-9 Queen Street, Portsmouth

Navy News

The Newspaper of The Royal Navy and The Royal Naval Association

No. 165, 14th YEAR, MARCH, 1968 — Published first Thursday of the month — Price One Shilling

MEET 'THE SEC.'

H.M.S. RESOLUTION HURLS FIRST U.K. MISSILE

POLARIS TEST FIRE 'PERFECT'

"Perfect in every respect" was the report when a Polaris missile was launched on February 15 from H.M.S. Resolution—the first time from a British submarine

New missile Project

'No burdens' promise

Admiralty's forecast on redundancy

HERMES HOME

Parkinson & Partners

FAREHAM

COWPLAIN

EMSWORTH

CHICHESTER

Navy News

OCTOBER 1979 10p

HERMES TO SAIL ON

SALUTE TO MOUNTBATTEN

WELL BRED!

Fife makes history in hurricane disaster

SHIPS ON SAFARI

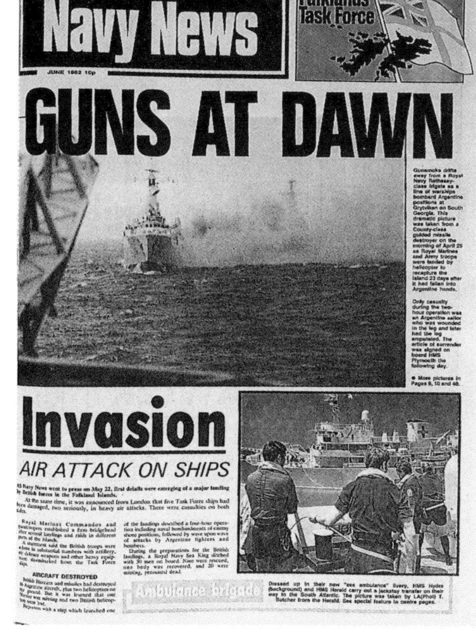

Navy News

Falklands Task Force

JUNE 1982 10p

GUNS AT DAWN

Invasion

AIR ATTACK ON SHIPS

Ambulance brigade

NN Navy News

MARCH 1991 20p

Deadly combination . . . . . . that devastated Saddam at sea

THE NAVY IN THE GULF

IRAQI NAVY WIPED OUT

OVER 40 Iraqi vessels have now been destroyed by the Allies — with a hefty share falling to Royal Navy helicopter pilots.

JACK-POT!

Diana at Drake

12 PER CENT — AND MORE

Gulf War 1991: a 846 Squadron Sea King hovers above a blazing oilfield in Kuwait – see page 102

THE Navy IN THE News 1954–1991

Jim Allaway

London: HMSO

First published 1993

ISBN 0 11 772753 9

Printed in the United Kingdom for HMSO
Dd 295591 C40 10/93 531/3 12521

The 1950s

1950 Royal Marine Barracks, Chatham closed.
HM Submarine Truculent sunk in Thames estuary after collision with SS Divine.
Royal Marine Bands integrated on formation of RM School of Music.
Start of UN operations in Korea.

1951 HMS Vidal launched – the first small ship designed to carry a helicopter and the first with cafeteria messing.
Court Martial Appeals Act passed.
Evacuation of Inchon, Korea.
RNR, RNVR and other reserves granted straight stripes.
Coupons introduced to ration duty-free tobacco.
HM Submarine Affray lost in the Channel.
Admiralty established Minewatching Services, forerunner of the RNXS.

1952 Ships expended in atomic tests at Monte Bello.
Clearance Diver Branch (Later MCD) formed.
First NATO Supreme Allied Commander Atlantic appointed.

1953 End of Korean War.
St Edward's Crown adopted for all epaulettes, badges and buttons.
Hawker Sea Hawk jet fighter entered service with 806 Naval Air Squadron at RNAS Brawdy.
First naval helicopter lift of troops into combat by RN Sikorskis in Malaya.

1954 The Queen first embarked in HMY Britannia.
First Royal Review of RNVR.
890 Naval Air Squadron reformed at RNAS Yeovilton with De Havilland Sea Venoms – the first turbo-jet all-weather Fleet Air Arm fighters.

1955 HMS Ark Royal – the 4th of name – commissioned, the first RN carrier built with an angled flight deck.
HMS Sidon sank in Portland Harbour after explosion of an experimental torpedo.
HMS Vidal formally annexed Rockall for Great Britain.

1956 'Boy' as rank or rating replaced by 'Junior'.
HMS Porpoise, the first new-style diesel-electric submarine launched at Barrow-in-Furness.
Blue caps worn for the last time.
White cap covers to be worn all year round.
Seamen, Engineer, Electrical and Supply Officers combined on the General List.
Plymouth Gunnery range at Wembury commissioned as HMS Cambridge.
The Suez Crisis

1957 HMS Centurion commissioned at Haslemere as Central Drafting authority.
Off caps at payment replaced by hand salute.
HMS Thorough returned to HMS Dolphin after first circumnavigation by a submarine.

1958 First flight of Westland Wasp helicopter.
RNR and RNVR combined to form the present RNR, RMFVR became RMR.
Last Naval Discipline Act came into force, Naval law thereafter deriving from the Armed Forces Acts.
HMS Eagle, Sheffield, Albion and Bulwark in emergency operations off Lebanon and Jordan.
First Royal Review of Fleet in Canadian waters.
First fishery dispute with Iceland over her unilateral extension of the fishing zone by 12 miles.
Closure of East Indies station – the oldest in permanent commission, it was absorbed by the Far East station.

1959 First of the highly successful Oberon class of conventional submarines launched at Chatham.
HM Dockyard Malta passed into civilian hands.
HM Dockyard Hong Kong closed.
Commander-in-Chief Home Fleet shifted flag ashore to Northwood, now HMS Warrior the HQ C-in-C Fleet.

The 1960s

Pages 14–29

1960	HMS Dreadnought, Britain's first nuclear-powered submarine, launched. Royal Marines, except recruits and bandsmen, empowered to wear the green beret of the Commandos. HMS Devonshire launched – first operational RN guided missile ship. RN Hospital Mauritius taken over from the Army (closed 1976). HMS Bulwark commissioned as the first Commando carrier. Sheerness closed as a naval dockyard. Agadir earthquake – HMS Tyne landed supplies and 60 wooden huts prefabricated onboard by her shipwrights. Death toll reported as 12,000 with over 20,000 left homeless.
1961	Closure of the Nore Command. End of first Cod War. Iraq threatened invasion of Kuwait. 42 Commando RM landed from HMS Bulwark. 45 Commando RM flown in from Aden. 815 Naval Air Squadron commissioned at RNAS Culdrose with Westland Wessex, the prototype Anti Submarine Warfare helicopter.
1962	RN Mine Watching Service renamed Royal Naval Auxiliary Service (RNXS).
1963	HMS Valiant, the first all-British designed nuclear submarine launched. First experimental "touch and go" by a Vertical Take Off/Landing aircraft on HMS Ark Royal off Portland.
1964	Last meeting of Board of Admiralty. The Queen assumed the title of Lord High Admiral of the United Kingdom when the Board of Admiralty became the Admiralty Board of the new Defence Council. 45 RM Commando landed at Dar-es-Salaam to suppress mutiny in Tanganyika Rifles. 45 Commando began operations in the Radfan.
1965	State Funeral of Sir Winston Churchill.
1966	Minewarfare and Clearance Diver Branch formed. HMS Lowestoft began the Beira Patrol off Mozambique as a result of Rhodesia's Unilateral Declaration of Independence. Maintained for nine years. HMS Resolution, the first British Polaris ballistic missile submarine launched. HMS Bristol, the first and last Type 82 destroyer ordered.
	Assault on Limbang, Brunei by L company 42 Commando RM – the first incident in the Indonesian Confrontation.
1967	Final withdrawal from Aden. South Atlantic and South American Station absorbed by Home Fleet. Home Fleet restyled Western Fleet. HMS Andromeda launched – the last ship built in Portsmouth Dockyard. Fleet Air Arm bombed wreck of Torrey Canyon, aground on the Longstones.
1968	HMS Scylla launched at Plymouth – the last ship to be built in a Royal Yard. NATO Standing Naval Force Atlantic (STANAVFORLANT) formed. First British Polaris missile fired from HMS Resolution, submerged 30 miles off Cape Kennedy. Closure of HMS St Vincent, boys training establishment at Gosport.
1969	HMS Amazon, the first Type 21 frigate, laid down. First Royal Marines deployment to Northern Ireland – 41 Commando on Spearhead duties. 892 Naval Air Squadron commissioned at RNAS Yeovilton – the only front line Fleet Air Arm squadron to be equipped with Phantom aircraft. RN Medical School at Alverstoke became the Institute of Naval Medicine. Commander-in-Chief Portsmouth became first C-in-C Naval Home Command. First helicopter deck landing, by a Westland Wessex, on RFA Engadine.

The 1970s

Pages 30–59

1970 Last tot issue.
First RN Hovercraft (BHN7) on trials at Lee-on-Solent.
824 Naval Air Squadron formed at Culdrose – the first operational deployment of Westland Sea King helicopters.
Revival of continuous commissioning of HM ships.
HMS Centurion commissioned at Gosport.

1971 Far East Fleet paid off (established 1946).
Commander-in-Chief Western Fleet became C-in-C Fleet.
Senior Naval Officer Persian Gulf hauled down his pennant.
HMS Sheffield, the first Type 42 destroyer launched (lost in the Falklands War).
First Fleet Chief Petty Officers appointed by warrant.
HM Submarine Artemis foundered alongside at Gosport.
HMS Swiftsure, first of new class of nuclear Fleet submarines, launched.

1972 RN Museum Portsmouth established.
End of Shipwright specialisation.
Formation of Commando Logistics Regiment, Royal Marines.
First plastic warship – the glass-reinforced plastic (GRP) minehunter HMS Wilton.
NATO Standing Naval Channel inaugurated at Ostend.
Anti-terrorist team including two Royal Marines parachuted into Atlantic alongside the QE2 to search for a reported bomb.

1973 Second Cod War – fishing dispute with Iceland when she unilaterally extended her fishing exclusion zone from 12 to 50 miles.
HMS Ariadne commissioned – the RN's last steam ship, she became the last to fire Limbo and the last RN ship to fire a broadside before she decommissioned in 1992. (A broadside, involves the firing of all guns on one side of the ship and the RN now has no twin turret ships).

1974 HMS Hermes, Andromeda and Rhyl evacuated British subjects from Kyrenia, Cyprus during Turkish invasion.

1975 Operations Branch formed.
Third Cod War, caused by Iceland's further extension of a 200 mile fishing limit.

1976 Post of QHM Scapa Flow abolished.
HMS Fittleton sunk in collision with Mermaid – 12 lives lost including ten RNR under training.
End of third Cod War.

1977 Royal Marines rigid raiding craft from HMS Vigilant captured five terrorists off Warrenpoint. Vigilant engaged shore positions.
WRNS subject to Naval Discipline Act.
New Meritorious Service Medal introduced for FCPOs, CPOs and POs.

1978 First deck landing by a Hawker Sea Harrier on HMS Hermes.
Phantom XT870/120 of 892 Naval Air Squadron catapulted from HMS Ark Royal – the end of conventional fixed wing flying in the RN.
Bahrein closed as a naval yard.

1979 Final withdrawal of RN from Malta.
HMS Ark Royal, the last fixed wing carrier until the advent of the ski-jump and the Harrier, paid off.
Murder of Admiral of the Fleet the Earl Mountbatten of Burma.

The 1980s

Pages 60–96

1980	HMS Invincible commissioned – the lead ship of the so called "through deck cruisers". HMS Glasgow in hurricane relief operations at St Lucia and Cayman Islands. Armilla Patrols began in the Gulf – HMS Coventry the first ship deployed. First Sea Harrier squadron, Naval Air Squadron 800, commissioned. Commachio Group RM formed. Established as a company and expanded in 1983, the unit has adopted many of 43 Commando's traditions. It provides extra security at Service establishments and installations and is skilled in maritime anti-terrorist work. RN's first hydrofoil, HMS Speedy, accepted.
1981	HMS Hermes recommissioned after being fitted with ski jump. Last parade of RN Division Old Association at Greenwich. English Harbour – "Nelson's Dockyard" – handed over to Antigua. HMS Ark Royal – the fifth of name – launched. Closure of Dauntless at Burghfield – WRNS training moved to HMS Raleigh at Torpoint. Faithful, the last paddle tug, paid off.
1982	The Falklands War – Operation Corporate.
1983	Admiral of the Fleet Lord Lewin nominated as the second Naval Knight of the Garter since Lord Howe. HMS Glamorgan and Brazen to Lebanon in support of British troops in multi-national force.
1984	Portsmouth Royal Dockyard relegated to Fleet Operational and Maintenance Base. RFA Reliant with Naval Party 2200 and 846 Naval Air Squadron evacuate 5,000 civilians from Lebanon. Chatham closed as a Naval dockyard.
1985	Demolition of RNEC Keyham.
1986	HMS Vernon decommissioned. HMY Britannia and HMS Newcastle, Jupiter and Hydra evacuate refugees from South Yemen. Last pay parade – at HMS Raleigh.
1987	HMS Warrior (1860), the Royal Navy's first ironclad, goes on permanent display at Portsmouth. HMS Norfolk, first Type 23 frigate, launched. Clearance divers help in rescue operations on Herald of Free Enterprise capsized off Zeebrugge. HMS Abdiel and four minehunters in Oman for a five month clearance of mines laid in Iran-Iraq War.
1988	HMS Abdiel, the last RN ship designed as a minelayer, paid off. HMS Fawn fired on by Guatemalan gunboats while surveying in Gulf of Honduras. Lynx helicopter from HMS Sirius fired on from Triton Island while rescuing crew from Taiwanese fishing boat. HMS Active and RFA Oakleaf in hurricane relief at Jamaica.
1989	Gangway staffs and upper deck carry arms.

The 1990s

Pages 97–105

1990	WRNS officers adopted RN ranks. Management of Naval Aviation came under one authority – Flag Officer Naval Aviation (FONA). Decision to send WRNS to sea announced.
1991	The Gulf War. RM and QARNNS deployed to SE Turkey and into Northern Iraq to provide humanitarian aid for Kurdish refugees. Royal Marine Barracks Eastney closed.
1992	HMS Vangard, first of the RN Trident submarines launched. Kit Upkeep Allowance abolished after 75 years. Malta Siege Bell Memorial dedicated at Valetta to the memory of 7,000 who died 10 June 1940 – 13 May 1943.

Foreword

by Admiral Sir Benjamin Bathurst GCB ADC
Chief of Naval Staff and First Sea Lord

Navy News and I joined the Navy about the same time and thus it gives me especial pleasure to see this superb newspaper approach its 40th birthday. The long list of awards it has won is a clear tribute to that excellence and in particular to its Editors.

This collection of photographs and stories is a splendid pastiche of the last four decades of immense change and challenge. During this period Navy News' readership has grown as the Navy's complement has reduced. This suggests to me that the level of interest in our affairs outside the serving Navy shows no sign of waning – and that helps keep us all on our toes.

Reading this book has brought back many memories for me, as I am sure it will for many of you – whether or not you have had the privilege of serving in the Royal Navy. But it is not just an exercise in nostalgia, for it shows clearly how far we have come.

I commend it to you and, on behalf of the Royal Navy and Royal Marines, would like to thank Navy News for keeping us in touch with one another as well as wishing all who work on the paper every success for the future.

Ben Bathurst

Acknowledgements

The first draft was over twice as long as could be comfortably and affordably contained within the format presented here. So a second volume – depending on the success of the first! – is already planned, while 'The Navy in the Nineties' looks likely to be a viable proposition for publication in these times of accelerating change that are already placing great demands on a smaller but ever more intensely professional 'Senior Service'.

Thanks to 'Nodge' Carnegie of HMSO for the design work; the editorial staff of Navy News, past and present, for the material on which the text is based; members of the RN Photographic Branch, whose pictures form the bulk of the illustrations; and Beryl Tullett, secretary to three successive Editors of Navy News, upon whose careful husbandry of our files this project has chiefly depended.

The Author

Jim Allaway became Editor of Navy News in February 1993. Educated at Portsmouth Southern Grammar School and the University of Kent, he joined the Government Information Service in 1978 and has since had two terms as Public Relations Officer to the Flag Officer Submarines. His biography of the Royal Navy's top submarine ace, Lieut.-Cdr David Wanklyn VC, DSO** 'Hero of the Upholder', was published in 1991.

The Humorists

'Tugg' Willson (top) and Charles Miles (below) in search of inspiration – between them these two talented cartoonists have put in 50 years on Navy News. See pages xi–xii.

Introduction

In compiling this book there was no idea of presenting a history of the modern Royal Navy – it was intended simply as a family album of pictures and memories. Since so many of our readers ask us for photographs of their old ships or information to settle arguments over time and place, it seemed to me that something of the sort might be welcome.

It could hardly satisfy everyone – there are bound to be many omissions and not a few units of the Fleet seem to have more than their fair share of the limelight. In justification of the selection offered here, I can only say that some of the famous names that recur again and again have done so through a combination of their own high profile public relations efforts and a hold on the popular imagination that sometimes might be said to transcend their actual performance.

HMS Ark Royal, in her two post-war incarnations, is a fair example. The present Ark has been a PR ship from the outset and her people have made the most of it – while her immediate predecessor enjoyed her last days as the chosen vehicle for "Sailor", still the most successful of all Naval TV documentaries.

I make no apology either for what might seem a more than equal showing accorded to the Submarine Service. In this period submarines, rendered truly independent by the application of nuclear power, came into their own as the supreme capital ships – though they perversely retain their original designation as submarine "boats". Their new status was underlined in the Falklands War, through the controversial sinking of the cruiser General Belgrano by HMS Conqueror. The rights and wrongs of this action have been hotly debated ever since, but the threat of a nuclear submarine presence effectively bottled up the Argentine Fleet thereafter and may have saved more lives than were lost on both sides.

Today the acquisition of submarines, both nuclear and conventional, by emergent nations with expansionist ambitions is seen to be a prime destabilising force even where motivated by purely local disputes – and the RN nuclear flotilla is poised to build on its potential, hitherto hardly realised thanks to the narrow preoccupations of the Cold War, as a long-range arm of British policy world-wide.

For the Royal Navy, the nuclear-powered submarine became the main striking arm of the Fleet in the era covered by this book – which exactly spans the arrival of the world's first, USS Nautilus, and the collapse of the Soviet Union, whose own submarine ballistic missile platforms set against those of the NATO powers formed the principal focus of the East-West arms race.

The political uncertainties that followed the demise of the Warsaw Pact, starkly exemplified by the turmoil in the Balkans and nationalist revivals in former Soviet republics whose separate identities were practically unknown in the West a year or two ago, go a long way to justify the continuance of the RN-operated independent nuclear deterrent, soon to be taken over by the Trident boats after a quarter of a century of unbroken patrols by the Polaris force.

First Sea Lord Admiral Sir Julian Oswald recently outlined a new approach to the Royal Navy's role – as part of a global police force,

countering the problems of drug trafficking, terrorism, piracy (on the ascendant, particularly in the Far East around Indonesia, as vicious and more ruthlessly efficient than in the days of Blackbeard and the Barbary Corsairs) and reinforcing a commitment to the maintenance of justice and fair dealing on the High Seas.

In many ways this marks a return to traditional practice – and "The Navy in the News" offers not a few examples of a side of business that continued to receive due attention during times when other considerations were presented as the RN's principal raison d'etre as part of the NATO alliance.

So to a small extent it does pretend to be a history of sorts – developments in ship design, naval aviation, organisational changes and wars and confrontations are featured here, along with the many occasions on which the Royal Navy and Royal Marines have been the prime (sometimes the sole) movers in disaster relief operations and mercy missions across the world. As economic considerations restrict opportunities for these – as, increasingly, it seems they must – the Royal Navy's availability for mounting humanitarian efforts of this kind will be sorely missed.

Warships are designed to fight and destroy – but in the spirit of Nelson's Prayer before Trafalgar, humanity in victory has been one of the proudest legacies of the Royal Navy's influence on warfare at sea. Sailors, whom one would expect to be hardened by their hard calling, are a notoriously soft touch when it comes to helping the disadvantaged. On runs ashore in foreign ports working parties give up their time to lend their many skills to charitable works. Almost all of these have to do with children – whether giving a lick of paint to an orphanage or organising parties in improvised fancy dress for visiting groups of underprivileged infants. I once witnessed one of these, when a little girl with both legs encased in calipers insisted on making her own way down the ladder of a submarine hatch. It took her a full half-hour – the supposedly hard-bitten matelots who had spent most of the previous night painting the town red after weeks on patrol patiently encouraging her every agonising step.

They have a natural empathy with any single-minded pursuit of excellence and achievement – and for nearly 40 years Navy News has recorded their support across a wide range of good causes.

The Royal Family has also figured strongly in these pages. Ever since the days of George V, a sailor king whose sense of duty and Empire was formed during his time at sea, the House of Windsor has been more intimately linked with the Senior Service than with any other branch of the Armed Services.

The Duke of Windsor was for long the Navy's most senior Admiral of the Fleet. Just before his abdication as Edward VIII his capacity for entrancing large crowds was never more evident, in the memory of Sir Samuel Hoare, as when he visited the Fleet at Portsmouth. A few weeks later, when George VI found himself saddled with a job for which he believed he was totally unprepared, he protested that he was "just a Naval officer" – and yet in a few short years when the world went to war he proved to have qualities that were exactly suited to the hour.

His daughter married a Naval officer and two of his grandchildren followed in the same tradition. HMS Bronington might have passed

into obscurity but for her connection with the Prince of Wales, while the Duke of York – who saw action in the Falklands – still continues his Naval career, latterly with his own first command, HMS Cottesmore. And it seems that hardly a month goes by without the Princess Royal's busy schedule including a visit in her capacity as Chief Commandant WRNS – a role of heightened importance as Wrens go to sea in increasing numbers. Navy News was founded in 1954 purely to serve the Portsmouth Command. Within a few months its success allowed it to expand to cover the whole of the Service. Today it has at least a quarter of a million readers – probably many more as we have plenty of evidence of how a few copies may be passed around whole ship's companies, ex-pat communities and ex-Service associations who use its columns to keep in touch with present developments and old shipmates. Our readers take a perverse delight in letting us know how many people they pass theirs on to – we would rather they bought their own! – but when it is realised that the total strength of the RN today is only around 55,000, it is clear that Navy News' influence spreads far beyond its first function as an in-house journal.

Foreign embassies and Press correspondents scan its pages, regularly picking up items they have missed through the usual lines of communication. Over the past 20 years it has collected over 60 awards in the competition run by the British Association of Industrial Editors – since 1972 in fact, not a year has gone by that has not seen some recognition for the excellence of its writing, design and photographic content.

Perhaps its most consistently appealing feature in this latter period has been its regular cartoon strip – for with Tugg Willson's 'Jack' Navy News acquired a character to rank with Fleet Street's comic immortals. 'Jack' first appeared in the February 1973 edition – and he is still with us today, frozen in rank and age as an AB of 20 or so, always the loser.

Though his failure over two decades to rise in his profession is hardly typical of today's increasingly highly qualified and motivated sailor, his ability to touch the sharp chord of RN humour, at once timeless and strongly contemporary, has never faltered.

This is, of course, a tribute to the evergreen vision of his creator, who left the Service in 1971 to concentrate on an already blossoming career as a cartoonist. Tugg was educated at the Royal Hospital School, Holbrook, and joined the Royal Navy as an armourer in 1947. In 1964 he received a commission on the Special Duties (Aviation) List and served all his sea time in carriers. His cartoons appear regularly in national newspapers and he works on commission for a number of companies, mainly in the maritime and aviation fields.

While the nuances of his wit are best appreciated by a Naval audience, Tugg seldom relies on "in jokes", though as the Prince of Wales – himself the subject of several of his sallies during his own Naval career – observed in a foreword to a collection we published in 1983; "If you have served in the Navy, then his cartoon characters are only too possible...he has the uncanny ability to evoke through his pen the kind of situations and personal characteristics that are so totally a part of the Royal Navy."

Several constant themes run through Jack's story. He is endlessly inventive in dreaming up excuses for not writing to his girl and equally adept at messing up a date – or his oppo's – with a few ill-chosen words.

The demise of the tot doesn't seem to have worried him much - but the day the WRNS ditched stockings and "sussys" in favour of tights deeply scarred his romantic soul.

Tugg Willson's genius in combining economy of line and caption – which is the essential figure of the cartoonist's art – is one of Navy News' greatest stylistic assets. But we rely even more on our other regular cartoonist, Charles Miles, who for 27 years has committed himself each month to half a dozen illustrations to lighten the official litany of Defence Council Instructions and Drafty pronouncements – plus a spread across the top of the leader page, offering an off-beat slant to the dominant issue of the day.

"Smiles", a former Lieutenant Commander who retired in 1988 after 24 years as Establishment Development Officer at HMS Dryad, began illuminating the dark corners of official communications in Navy News in 1966. Since then he has produced over 2,000 cartoons poking gentle – and sometimes not so gentle – fun at Naval characters and institutions. In 1990 the BAIE introduced a special award for humour – and he at once picked up a Certificate of Merit.

Many of the photographs in this collection are unique – whether they be amateur snapshots submitted by members of ships' companies or pictures specially commissioned from the Royal Navy's own Photographic Branch, they have appeared nowhere else but in the pages of Navy News, whose archive is one of the most complete pictorial records of the Senior Service in the post war era. A good many of them bring back memories to one who has had the privilege over 15 years of recording the activities of the branch of the Armed Services with which the British people have always identified most closely. I hope they do the same for you.

Today the Royal Navy has more ongoing commitments at home and overseas – with far fewer units to maintain them – than it did 20 years ago. In such circumstances it will ever be a "Navy in the News."

Jim Allaway
Old Portsmouth
September, 1993

The 1950s

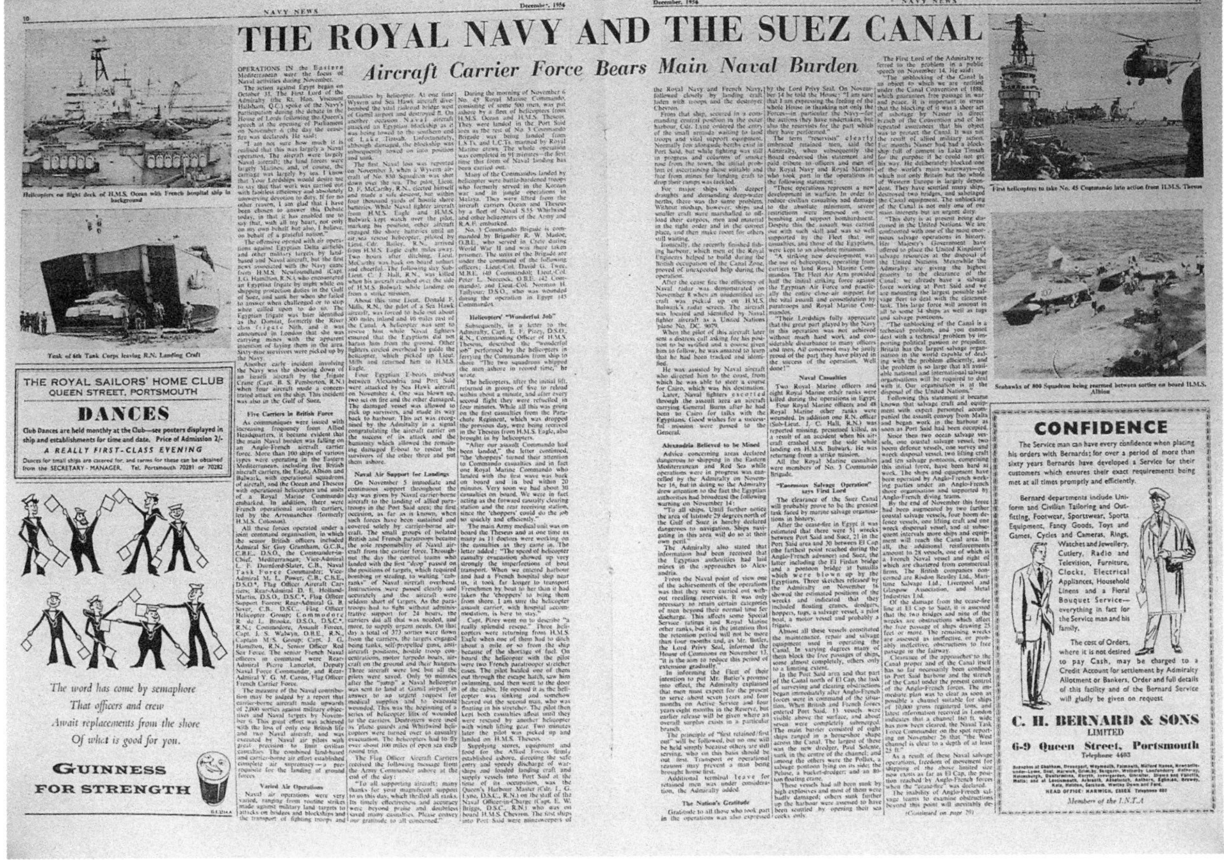

NAVY NEWS December, 1956

THE ROYAL NAVY AND THE SUEZ CANAL

Aircraft Carrier Force Bears Main Naval Burden

Helicopters on flight deck of H.M.S. Ocean with French hospital ship in background

Tank of 6th Tank Corps leaving R.N. Landing Craft

First helicopters to take No. 45 Commando into action from H.M.S. Theseus

Seahawks of 800 Squadron being rearmed between sorties on board H.M.S. Albion

(Continued on page 29)

Early Days on Navy News

1

4

2

1 *Special offer – Bulwark and the Beverley Sisters*

The first issue of Navy News, in June 1954, featured the commissioning of HMS Albion, an aircraft carrier of the Hermes class, at Wallsend-on-Tyne. Launched seven years earlier by Mrs Attlee, wife of the first post-war Labour Prime Minister, her flight deck, angled 5½ degrees to port, reflected the rapid development of jet aircraft which required a landing area clear forward with no safety barriers. Six months later she was followed by HMS Bulwark – seen here as she looked then, the subject of the first of a long series of postcards issued by Navy News, and 27 years later when she paid off for the last time.

"It is no easy task to design a carrier which can cope with the constant and rapid development of aircraft," the paper commented. "Ten years ago Sea Furies, Corsairs and Hellcats were considered pretty fast with a top speed of around 300 knots; today Sea Hawks and Sea Venoms double that speed."

The keel of the Hermes class aircraft carrier had been laid down ten years before, but with the end of hostilities work on her was slowed down and she was not launched until 1948 – by Countess Granville, sister of the Queen Mother. The outbreak of the Korean War finally acted as a spur to her completion.

Also on offer in this first December edition were autographed photographs of a trio of winsome young girl singers who were to enjoy a resurgence of popularity 35 years later: "If you would like the Beverley Sisters for Christmas, write c/o The Portsmouth Navy News." [*December 1954*]

2 *Bulwark's Farewell*

Tugs, PAS boats and other small craft escort the Bulwark as, with paying off pennant flying, she bids her last farewell to Gibraltar. [April *1981*]

3 Bye, bye blues

HMS Victory staff get up to date with issue No 7 of what was then still the Portsmouth Navy News. Note the blue caps, worn from October to April until 1956, when the white covers used in the warmer months would henceforth be retained all year round. [*December 1954*]

3

4 On the buses

HMS Stickleback, first of the new improved descendants of the famous X-Craft midget submarines that attacked the Tirpitz in Kaafjord, Norway in September 1943, was launched at Barrow-in-Furness .

The Board of Admiralty had decided to give them "the names of the smaller denizens of the waters" and Stickleback, originally designated X 51, was quickly followed by HMS Shrimp. The originals were powered by diesel engines of the type used to drive London Transport buses. [*February 1955*]

5 Cumberland takes a shower

Today's young sailors, newly introduced to anti-nuclear procedures, may not realise that their fathers – and not a few of their grandfathers – went through similar drills. The trials cruiser HMS Cumberland is carrying out "pre-wetting" tests designed to be employed by ships operating in the fall-out area or the outer fringe of a region affected by an atomic explosion.

"The method involves the continual washing of all weather surfaces of the ship during and after exposure. Experiments have shown that fission matter is less likely to adhere to a surface while it is subjected to a system of salt water washdown. While the system is operating, the ship's company remains under cover and continues to control weapons and 'cons' the ship from between decks. All openings are closed and would remain so until conditions on the upper decks have been ascertained by Geiger counter. 'Our aim was to produce a rainstorm of tropical intensity,' said an officer in charge of the sprays fitted around the ship." [*November 1955*]

6 Bird artist's Grey Goose

HMS Grey Goose was a steam gunboat in which Lieutenant Commander Peter Scott, MBE, DSC and Bar, RNVR – the celebrated artist and naturalist who was the son of Captain Scott of Antarctic fame – led a series of dashing Channel actions against enemy shipping in World War II.

These "destroyers in miniature" had powerful steel hulls, a three-inch gun, torpedoes and depth charges and their 8,000 hp high efficiency steam turbines fired from a single boiler gave them a speed of 35 knots – but they were described as 'light coastal craft' and the enemy was left to assume that they were ordinary motor gun and torpedo boats.

The Grey Goose is here under the command of Lieutenant Commander D W Wilson DSM, RN, converted to a floating test bed with two experimental Rolls Royce RM 60 marine gas turbines, transmitting their power through ROTOL controllable pitch propellors which obviated the use of reverse gearing – alterations almost amounting to a rebuild. [*December 1955*]

6

5

7 *Crabb legend lingers on*

The Skoryi class destroyer Smotryashchy enters Portsmouth Harbour, accompanying the cruiser Ordzhonikidze for the visit of the Russian leaders chiefly remembered for the mysterious disappearance of Cdr Lionel "Buster" Crabb while allegedly spying under the hull of the latter. A headless and handless corpse dredged up in Chichester Harbour over a year later was identified by a close colleague as that of the celebrated wartime frogman, but later investigations have disputed this and reported sightings of Crabb behind the Iron Curtain have kept the legend alive ever since. [*May 1956*]

7

Commander L. K. P. Crabb, O.B.E., G.M.

8 *Sea Slug seen boxing clever*

With her high-walled, boxy superstructure HMS Girdle Ness, newly commissioned as the Royal Navy's first guided missile ship, looked an unlikely test-bed for the later generation of slim-line frigates for whom the gun would be a secondary armament. She began her career as a trials ship at Devonport in July 1956 and is seen (below) firing Sea Slug – a weapon that would remain in service for years – from her fo'c'sle in the summer of the following year.

8

8a

Naval interest in guided weapons started in World War II and the Royal Navy was in the forefront of their development in the period 1943–49. During the war an Admiralty committee was set up to investigate means of providing the Pacific Fleet with a short-range guided weapon to counter Kamikaze attacks – but Japan was defeated before the project was sufficiently advanced.

After tests at the Aberporth range in Wales and at Woomera in Australia and firings at sea – the majority of which were successful – the Sea Slug system was introduced. It was designed to engage any enemy bomber which managed to evade the fighter defences of the Fleet at any height at which aircraft were then capable of operating and employed four boosts, jettisoned after propelling the missile to supersonic speed. [*October 1956*]

9

9 *Cool Britannia*

By now home in Portsmouth after what was then the longest cruise ever undertaken by a Royal Yacht, HMY Britannia is seen here near Port Lochroy during the Duke of Edinburgh's tour of the Antarctic. She had left the UK on August 28 of the previous year to log 39,500 miles, rounding both the Cape of Good Hope and Cape Horn. Princess Margaret was embarked for an earlier part of the cruise, from Mombassa to Mauritius and Zanzibar and back to Dar-es-Salaam. Then the Queen and the Duke joined her to attend the Olympic Games at Melbourne, visiting the Seychelles, Ceylon, Malaya and New Guinea.

After calling at Tristan da Cunha and St Helena – where a rating had the chance to revisit his homeland – and Ascension Island, Prince Philip was taken 80 miles up the Gambia River for the annual Chiefs Conference at Sankewla [*March 1957*]

10 *Carrier-borne cat-napper*

The carrier HMS Eagle's newly acquired mascot sees in the New Year in a made-to-measure hammock, comfortably getting into the swing of shipboard life. Pets are no longer permitted in HM ships. [*January 1957*]

10

11 *Upon the face of the waters*

While operating her aircraft in an exercise in Scottish waters HMS Ark Royal ran into heavy weather. The sea broke over the flight deck after three Sea Hawk Jet fighters had been recovered. There were five more in the air – but all were brought in safely. Two other carriers operating with the Ark also had several of their aircraft in the air at the time and while an undercarriage or two were damaged no-one was hurt. Decks were rising and falling 40-50ft at their extremities. [*February 1958*]

11

12 *Mass fly-past over Malta*

In this month the Ark put up her Sea Venom and Sea Hawk fighters for a mass fly-past over Malta. Here the Sea Hawks fire their starting cartridges before being launched by catapult. [*February 1958*]

12

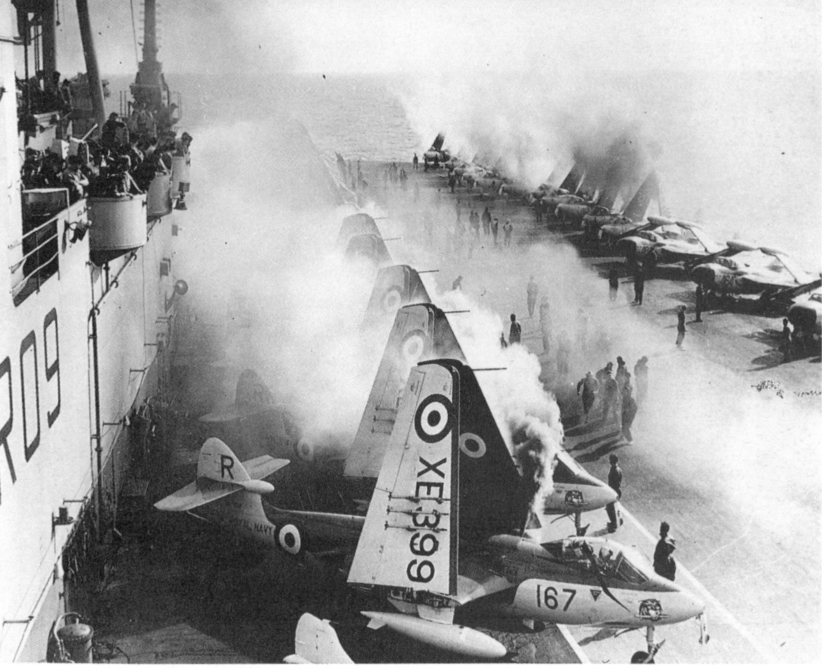

13 **Noisy Scimitar sweeps low**

The Royal Navy's new interceptor fighter, the swept wing Scimitar, was soon to come into service. This large single seater aircraft had an exceptional low level performance and was capable of supersonic speed in shallow dives. The first squadron was formed at RN Air Station Lossiemouth in June 1958 and was expected to embark in the Navy's newly modernised carrier HMS Victorious the following September. "A feature of the airplane not appreciated by people living near RN Air Station Ford in West Sussex where it was recently demonstrated, was its terrific noise..." [*April 1958*]

13

14

14 **Shiny Sheff talks Turkey**

HMS Sheffield, veteran of the Bismarck fight, fires a salute to the President of Turkey, 150 miles south of Malta.

The "Shiny Sheff" – whose name would he perpetuated with the arrival of a Type 22 frigate in 1988 – also included Norway, Spartivento, the Atlantic, Mediterranean, Malta Convoys, Arctic, North Africa, Barents Sea, Salerno. Biscay and North Cape in her Battle Honours. [*April 1958*]

15 **Protector provides cold comfort**

Frozen spray on HMS Protector (below) in Bransfield Strait, between the South Shetlands and Graham Land, Antarctica. The converted fast net layer commissioned for work as the guardship to the Governor of the Falkland Islands and Dependencies returned home to Portsmouth having steamed over 38,500 miles in seven and a half months. During her time down south the survey ship HMS Shackleton was damaged in ice off the South Orkney Islands and Protector sailed at speed to meet her, carried out temporary repairs and escorted her back to South Georgia. Shipwright Sub Lieut GH Avery and LS R Woodhouse spent three hours in water near freezing point fixing a plate over the holes to make her seaworthy for the 600 mile trip. On her last tour of the Dependencies survey bases the Protector moved 16 Husky dogs, ten men and $7\frac{1}{2}$ tons of stores from Livingstone Island to Hope Bay on the NE coast of Graham Land – all by helicopter. "The dogs made admirable aircraft passengers..." [*June 1958*]

15

16 **Eyeball to eyeball in Albion**

All this and a hangar-full too! – the uplift of nearly 500 military vehicles in HMS Albion was officially declared a record. At the time of the assassination of Iraq's Royal Family the carrier was working up her squadrons in Scottish waters. Very soon she was ordered to proceed south to the Channel area. On arrival her aircraft were flown off to their parent stations and within three days she sailed from Portsmouth with over 1,000 eye bolts welded to the flight deck to tie the vehicles down. A large number of military personnel, including the whole of No 42 RM Commando, were also embarked. Four days later she arrived at Malta.

The threat of war had sent HMS Bermuda to Tobruk where she was joined by the Dispatch Vessel Surprise and the anti-submarine frigate HMS Torquay. Forces were taken from Gibraltar to Benghazi in HMS Cumberland. HMS Bulwark was at Mombasa, whence she embarked troops to Aden. [*September 1958*]

17

16

17 **Air power for Brave Borderer**

HMS Brave Borderer, undergoing trials at Vosper's, Portsmouth, was the first of two new fast patrol boats – Brave Swordsman was the other – "which will help to keep alive Coastal Forces techniques in the Royal Navy". Carrying four 21 inch torpedoes and a Bofors gun, she had a complement of three officers and 17 ratings and her three Marine Proteus gas turbines gave her a speed of over 50 knots. These had been adapted from engines used in the Britannia aircraft. [*February 1959*]

18 **Ugly ducking once a swan**

HMS Tiger, the Navy's first new cruiser to enter service in 15 years, was actually laid down in 1941. Work on her stopped at the end of hostilities and was not resumed until the wartime cruisers reached the end of their lives. Then, after substantial redesign work, she rejoined the Fleet to a mixed reception. The days of conventional cruisers bristling with heavy guns were numbered – despite the "phenomenally high rate of fire" of the three inch fully automatic batteries and the six-inch weapons that loosed off shells three times faster than any other guns of that calibre.

In December 1966 Tiger gained lasting fame as the venue for the 'Tiger Talks' between Prime Minister Harold Wilson and the Rhodesian Premier Ian Smith at the time of the unilateral declaration of independence of the country that would eventually emerge as Zimbabwe.

After a four-year refit costing a then astronomical £13.25m, she reappeared in 1972 carrying four Sea King antisubmarine helicopters tightly packed in a box-like hangar which earned her the nickname 'Ugly Duckling'. Her last commanding officer, Cdr Mike Thomas commented: "It is sobering to realise that in all that time (38 years) she has spent less than 14 years on operational service and steamed a very modest total of 400,000 miles."

This photograph gives an idea of her earlier clean lines, power and speed. [*March 1959*]

18

19

19 **Andrew stars with Ava and Fred**

HMS Andrew had a leading role in 'On the Beach', Stanley Kramer's bleak film of the world ending not with a bang but a whimper as nuclear fallout slowly edges south to Australia. Taken from the novel by Nevil Shute, it starred Gregory Peck as the commander of USS Sawfish, falling half in love with Ava Gardner as he struggles to come to terms with the loss of his family back home in the United States where all human life is already extinct.

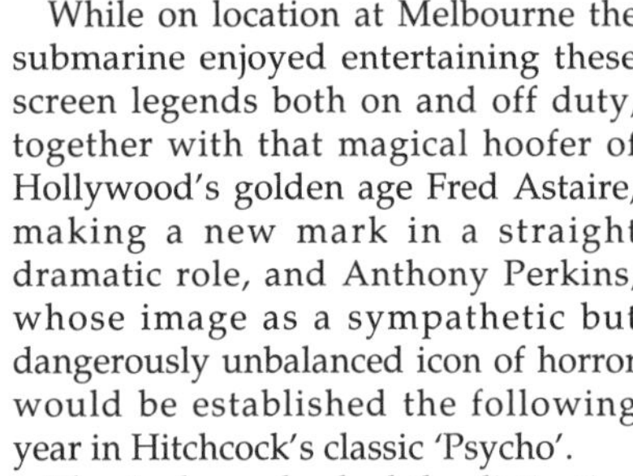

While on location at Melbourne the submarine enjoyed entertaining these screen legends both on and off duty, together with that magical hoofer of Hollywood's golden age Fred Astaire, making a new mark in a straight dramatic role, and Anthony Perkins, whose image as a sympathetic but dangerously unbalanced icon of horror would be established the following year in Hitchcock's classic 'Psycho'.

The Andrew also had the distinction of being the first vessel to fly the new 49-starred US flag – the State of Alaska did not come into being for another five months, so this was at least one authentic piece of prophesy. She would also be the last Royal Navy submarine to mount a gun, now preserved on the jetty of the Alma Mater of the Submarine Service, HMS Dolphin at Gosport, Hants. [*April 1958*]

20

20 **Learning the family business**

The young Prince Charles already seems to be adopting a proprietorial air as he watches CPO Rounding repair drop tanks on board HMS Eagle. Eighteen years later he would have his own command, the minesweeper HMS Bronington. He spent several hours on board the carrier as she steamed down Channel from Weymouth, taking the wheel for a time as she came to full speed. [*May 1959*]

21

21 Handsome is as handsome never did

On October 9, 1959 it had been announced that the 44,500 ton battleship HMS Vanguard, the last of Britain's 'Ships of the Line', would be scrapped. She had been the Reserve Fleet headquarters ship at Portsmouth since 1956, but the enormous cost of maintaining her made it obvious that her disposal was only a matter of time. Launched in 1944 and completed in 1946, too late for World War II, the largest warship ever built in Great Britain never fired a shot in anger. Her 15 inch guns were first mounted in HMS Courageous and HMS Glorious in 1917. She is remembered mainly for the Royal Tour to South Africa, February-May 1947 – but was recognised as the one of the most handsome ships the Royal Navy ever had. *[November 1959]*

22 Hermes the modernised Centaur

Undergoing full power trials in the Channel prior to her acceptance is HMS Hermes, the Royal Navy's newest carrier which commissioned on November 25. The first of the Hermes (modernised) class – to distinguish her from the Centaur class of which she was originally a sister ship – her aircraft complement included Super-Marine Scimitar strike fighters, de Havilland Sea Vixen all-weather fighters fitted with Firestreak air-to-air missiles, Westland Whirlwind anti-submarine helicopters and a flight of Fairey Gannet airborne early warning aircraft. *[December 1959]*

22

The 1960s

Navy News

The Newspaper of The Royal Navy and The Royal Naval Association

No. 165, 14th YEAR, MARCH, 1968 Published first Thursday of the month Price One Shilling

MEET 'THE SEC.'

It still comes as some surprise that "The Sec" may be a Wren officer. 2/O Patricia Anne Ewing (left), who has already served in Malta, is going to Mauritius as secretary to the commanding officer and officer-in-charge of the Wrens. Her place as secretary to the captain at H.M.S. Phoenix is being taken by 3/O Josephine Susan Wilkes (right), who has a double "appointment," having just become engaged to Surg. Lieut. Neil Attenborough.

H.M.S. RESOLUTION HURLS FIRST U.K. MISSILE

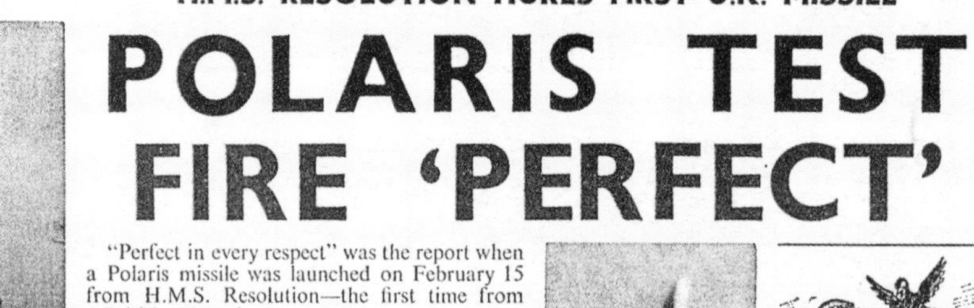

POLARIS TEST FIRE 'PERFECT'

"Perfect in every respect" was the report when a Polaris missile was launched on February 15 from H.M.S. Resolution—the first time from a British submarine.

The nuclear-powered Resolution was cruising submerged about 30 miles off Cape Kennedy, Florida, when she hurled the Polaris to the target area down the Atlantic Missile Test Range.

Watchers from attendant vessels saw a swirl of green water. Seconds later the missile burst through the surface in a fountain of foam.

The firing was carried out by the Port Crew under Cdr. Michael Henry. Watching were some of the Starboard Crew and their commanding officer, Cdr. Kenneth Frewer.

Cdr. Frewer and his crew later took over Resolution to begin preparations for the second test this month.

Vice-Admiral Sir Hugh Mackenzie, Chief Polaris Executive, who was on board Resolution, radioed after the firing:

"The event is the culmination of a great effort on the part of the submarine commanding officer and his crew, and by the British shipyards, firms and technicians who have built and tested the submarine and its systems.

"It has also set one more example of the efficiency of the Polaris weapons system, which was designed, developed and perfected in the United States of America."

On her return to Cape Canaveral, Resolution was piped into the dock by L/Cpl. David Cairns, of the Royal Scots Greys.

At six-monthly intervals during the next two years the other Polaris submarines, as they become operational, will make the same test firings. Thereafter the submarines will cross the Atlantic once a year, giving ship's companies a popular run ashore in the sunshine and attractions of Florida.

New missile Project

A naval close-range self-defence surface-to-air guided weapon is among the major development projects mentioned in the Defence White Paper. It is known as PX 430.

The existing Seacat missile has been claimed as having capability in countering such weapons as the Soviet Styx missile, which sank the Israeli destroyer Elath last October.

A development of Seacat would not only increase its value for dealing with close flying aircraft, but as an anti-missile missile.

"Never mind the pigeons. It's the cuckoos down below who worry me!"

'No burdens' promise

Cuts in the armed forces are not going to mean heavier burdens for those who remain, according to the pledge by the Government in the Defence White Paper.

"It has been a fundamental principle of the current examination," said the White Paper, "that reductions in capability, whether in terms of manpower or equipment, must be accompanied by reductions in the tasks imposed by the commitments that we require the Services to undertake.

"We have no intention of allowing a repetition of the situation which existed in 1964 when, because of the lack of balance between military tasks and resources, our forces were seriously overstretched."

The White Paper [illegible] that [illegible] document [illegible] intention to present [illegible] a Supplementary Statement.

Admiralty's forecast on redundancy

As promised in the February issue of "Navy News," the Admiralty Board have produced with all possible speed an assessment of the redundancy situation consequent on the Government's latest defence decisions.

"Withdrawing from east of Suez by the end of 1971," says a statement to the Fleet, "means reducing the strength of the Navy by about 16,000 officers and ratings in a period of five years instead of eight.

"We estimate that about three-quarters of this reduction will be achieved by adjusting entries, reducing fifth and sixth five and NCS engagements, discharges of time-expired officers and men and losses due to sickness, voluntary retirements, compassionate discharges and discharges by purchase.

"The remaining quarter of the reduction, that is about 4 per cent of our present overall strength of officers and men (though not evenly spread between differing ranks and ratings) will have to be obtained by compulsory premature discharges, namely redundancy.

"Due to the phasing out of fixed-wing aircraft and aircraft carriers, much of this must regrettably be borne by officers and ratings in the Fleet Air Arm.

"Before we can identify these numbers in more precise detail there is much work to be done. We hope, however, that enough progress will have been made by next [illegible] estimate which we intend to promulgate as soon as this is possible.

"Because we cannot make any large reductions until the withdrawals from east of Suez are well under way, few redundancy discharges will occur during the next three years.

"This means that, having worked out the numbers who must be discharged as redundant, there will be time to call for volunteers."

HERMES HOME

Happy family reunion for AB Ken Burge, wife Maureen, and little Paula when H.M.S. Hermes returned to Portsmouth from the Far East. Their home is at Ebbw Vale (Mon.).

(See also page 19)

23

24

25

23 **Long odyssey of Telemachus**

HMS Telemachus at Aden, on her way home after ten years' yeoman service with the Fourth Submarine Squadron in Australia and New Zealand. She arrived at Portsmouth on 9 December. With her complement of five officers and 57 ratings she had steamed 276,742 miles since her completion in 1943 and had visited most of the ports in the Pacific and Far East. In 1949 she had been the founder member of the newly formed Fourth Squadron. She was the last of the three T-Class submarines to return and in that time she had run for five commissions and completed four major refits at Singapore. [*January 1960*]

24 **Aftermath of maelstrom in Mauritius**

After a year's foreign service in the Mediterranean, Far East and South Africa Stations, the cruiser HMS Gambia, seen here at Cape Town – returned to Portsmouth at the end of her last commission. She had been at Mauritius in March, lending a hand in the aftermath of the cyclone disaster. [*July 1960*]

25 **Hardy souls return to Narvik**

The ninth HMS Hardy at Narvik, scene of her famous predecessor's celebrated action of April 10, 1940. Then the Second Destroyer Flotilla – the 7th Hardy leading Hunter, Havoc, Hotspur and Hostile – surprised a large force of German destroyers by entering the Norwegian harbour undetected and sinking two of the enemy and six merchant ships. When making their getaway they inflícted heavy damage on three more destroyers – but had their retreat cut off further down the fjord.

In the fierce battle that ensued HMS Hardy, her bridge and steering gear wrecked, was beached and her commanding officer, Warburton-Lee, was later posthumously awarded the first VC of the war. A hundred and fifty survivors were cared for by the inhabitants of nearby Ballangen and rescued by HMS Ivanhoe three days later during the Second Battle of Narvik.

Now a Type 14 frigate of the Second Frigate Squadron based at Portland was berthed at a jetty which once accommodated a German destroyer her illustrious forebear had torpedoed and sunk. On board was Lieut.-Cdr G R Heppel, RN (Retd) flotilla, torpedo officer in the seventh Hardy.

During the four-day visit wreaths were laid on the British War Memorial at Narvik and on Warburton-Lee's grave at Ballangen. [*October 1960*]

26 **Belfast shuttle**

HMS Belfast, the Royal Navy's biggest cruiser, (then the flagship of the Flag Officer Second-In-Command Far East Station Rear Admiral Michael Le Fanu), recommissioned at Singapore under the command of Captain Morgan Giles. The new crew, 52 officers and 580 men, were flown out in seven flights of specially commissioned Britannia aircraft of British United Airways and the British Overseas Airways Corporation while the old crew flew back home after 18 months' service in the Far East. [*March 1961*]

27 **Send her Victorious**

HMS Victorious makes a big impression as she leaves harbour, her ship's company lining the flight deck with an array of Scimitar, Sea Vixen and Gannet aircraft. [*September 1961*]

26

27

28a

28 **Tristan's sad tale well told**

HMS Leopard's 1600 mile dash across the South Atlantic from Simonstown, the naval base in South Africa, to the stricken island of Tristan da Cunha, produced one of the best pieces of reportage Navy News has ever carried – by an unidentified member of her ship's company.

Hastily loaded with 16 tons of emergency stores – everything from blankets to six-inch nails, tarpaulins to split peas – she sped off to a pinpoint on the chart reported to be in the throes of a volcanic eruption "that could have been about to disappear in the best Krakatoa-type fashion."

The disturbances had begun in August as earth tremors of varying intensity. Rock falls from the cliffs had continued until October 8, when cracks appeared in the ground at the eastern end of the settlement. The volcano finally erupted two days later – and by the afternoon of October 12 all 257 inhabitants had been put on the Dutch liner Tjisadane and sent off to Cape Town. HMS Leopard passed her on the way – most of the crew lining the port side to cheer the bewildered refugees.

28b

"It was a touching scene as we parted in the gathering gloom, us not knowing quite what to expect at Tristan and the islanders not knowing quite what to expect at Cape Town. At 1000 on Friday 13, a dark cloud on the horizon began to take shape which soon could be identified as the 7,000 ft cone of Tristan da Cunha, at a distance of 40 miles. As we approached, the world's loneliest island subtly rose out of the sea ahead. It was not until we were 15 miles off that we could see smoke rising from the northern edge...

"Nestling at the foot of a 2,000 ft cliff at the back of the settlement was what looked like a Black Country slag heap that was emptying a column of white smoke into the air. It was only when one looked down to the canning factory at the water's edge that one realised how large the cone was. To the

right was a cluster of crofts which formed the settlement, and below them on the green slope which extended from the base of the cliffs were white bungalows. We could see cattle grazing quietly in the fields and the sea birds wheeling in flight about us. All was quiet and peaceful, the air of drama being given by the pall of smoke that hung in the breeze..." HMS Leopard's task was to salvage valuable and personal belongings, embark the heavy gear from the canning factory and destroy the island's dog population.

"The saddest tale was told by the dog destruction party. The original plan had been to round up the dogs and shoot them through their heads as painlessly as possible. Unfortunately, after the first few had been despatched, the dogs all became timid and would not come near the party. It was found by painful experience that the .22 rifles were not sufficient to kill a dog outright from any range, and so the destruction had to be stood over until the next day when a party of marksmen could be landed with .303 rifles.

"The dogs were all of the collie type. At a guess I would say that they were crosses between alsatian and collie. I found that to shoot a dog even with a heavy calibre rifle at close range required an immense concentration to keep a steady hand. After the dog was dead, a feeling of nausea prevailed and it was necessary to remind myself that it was an essential task if the island was to be of any value in time to come."

Two ten-week-old puppies were spared to be taken on board the Leopard – where they were duly christened 'Tristan' and 'Cunha'. Some 200 sheep and cattle were left behind – and a stock of tinned food for the use of fishermen who might call as they plied the crayfish trade around the island. "We sailed at dark, taking a last look at the glowing volcano where the rocks were now reaching the path down to the canning factory and getting close to the first cottages... The trip back to Cape Town was made more interesting by all-out efforts to raise a fund for the islanders so that they would have some spending money on their trip to the United Kingdom. When the total in the fund had been counted, it was found that we had raised £235, an average of more than £1 per man." [*December 1961*]

28c

29 Fifty bridegrooms flooded with relief

The carrier HMS Victorious arriving at Mombasa to help in the Kenya flood relief programme. Her helicopters operated a 'flying doctor' service and casualty evacuation operation from a specially constructed jungle heliport.

When she returned to Portsmouth after nearly a year's service East of Suez, she had steamed 83,000 miles, spending 222 days out of 333 away at sea. For three months Victorious had stood by for the Kuwait emergency, logging 30,000 miles in the extreme heat of a Persian Gulf summer. In the 92 days of her stand-by, she was at sea for 75 – a high rate of seatime even by wartime standards. Included in her ship's company were no less than 50 prospective bridegrooms who were expecting to tie the knot during the leave period. [*January 1962*]

29

30

30 Squadron steams off station

In the pre-war, piping days of peace, ships used to leave their home ports for a Foreign Commission of about 2½years. They would spend the whole time on the station to which they were sent and a destroyer squadron worked together, in the main, as a unit. Times had changed – the First Destroyer Squadron (Saintes, Solebay and Finisterre, seen here with Camperdown astern) was paying off for the last time after two years in which the units had seen little of their base at Malta, either singly or together. Their duties had taken them from the Persian Gulf to the West African coast and they had visited ports in almost every country between.

HMS Solebay paid the first warship visit to Cyprus since the island became a republic and was made very welcome – some libertymen had to rejoin off the north coast after a long journey by truck and jeep, chasing the ship all day. Solebay and Saintes acted as Royal Escort for the Queen's State Visit to Italy and for the Duke of Gloucester's tour of the war graves in Greece and Turkey in the Royal Yacht.

When the Kuwait crisis blew up the squadron – minus Solebay, which was alongside refitting – was despatched to the area. They escorted the carrier Centaur through the Suez Canal to the Persian Gulf via Aden. All three spent long periods at sea in very hot weather and did not see the Mediterranean again until shortly before the squadron returned to the UK.

"In the meantime Solebay was defending the far-flung outposts of the Empire by visiting Corfu (cricket and ginger beer), Venice (sultry romance), and Dubrovnik (Yugoslavia culture again!)."

During a visit to Corfu, Solebay was visited by the King and Queen of Greece, the Crown Prince and Princesses of Greece and Don Juan, his wife, daughter and son, Don Carlos, of Spain, who were holidaying in the island.

Solebay and Saintes were again selected to undertake escort duties for the Queen's tour of West Africa. Joining the Royal Yacht at Takoradi, she paid visits to Monrovia, Freetown and Bathurst.

"We have dressed ship overall 36 times, steamed thousands of miles and lost only three bachelors in foreign ports..." [*April 1962*]

31 Scarborough speeds off to the sun

HMS Scarborough, the Whitby Class anti-submarine frigate, under helm at speed. She was glad to leave the freezing British winter for six months in the Mediterranean. From Gibraltar she moved to La Spezia in Northern Italy – which afforded daily bus tours to Florence and Pisa: "There are now over a hundred of us who stood at the top of the Leaning Tower... From La Spezia we moved on to Aranci Bay in Sardinia, where we joined up with the rest of the Mediterranean Fleet for concentrated exercises before going on to Malta... in the throes of an election while we were there, but all seemed to pass off peacefully, and the island has her own government again after being without one for five years."

On February 26 Scarborough had rendezvoused with the Royal Yacht to escort the Princess Royal on her visits to Famagusta and Limassol in Cyprus, and to Tobruk. [*May 1962*]

31

32

33

32 **Blake still banging on**

The cruiser HMS Blake fires her six-inch guns. The ship's main armament in this age of missile technology still consisted of four medium calibre guns mounted in two twin turrets. Their rate of fire was twenty rounds per minute – more than twice that of any previous cruiser. [*July 1962*]

33 **Rare brood**

"Some Ducklings" – an unusual picture of a rare occurrence. No less than 15 submarines alongside the submarine depot ship HMS Adamant at Falmouth during a 'wash-up' after exercises. [*October 1962*]

34

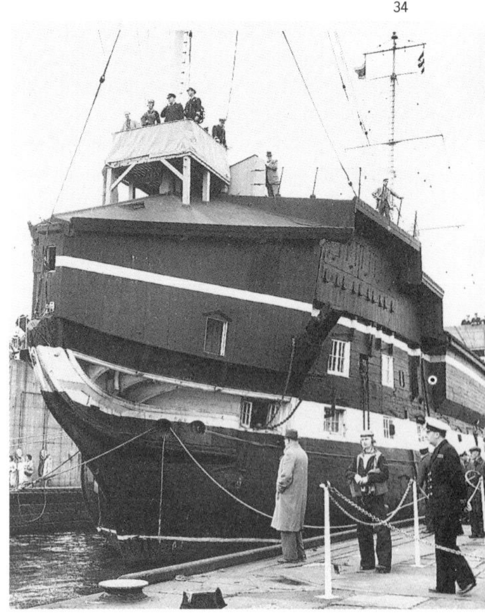

34 *Unicorn horns in just behind schedule*

For the first time since she arrived at Dundee's Earl Grey Dock in 1873, the old wooden wall frigate Unicorn was on the move. The longtime headquarters of Tay Division Royal Naval Reserve's continued existence was threatened by plans for the approach to the projected Tay Road Bridge, which necessitated the filling in of her abode. Doubts had been expressed over her ability to stand up to a shift to a new location and for a time it appeared she might be broken up – even blown up! – on the spot. When a new home at the other end of Dundee Harbour was identified and the commanding officer of the Division, Captain Peter Sime, director of a local timber concern, was able to provide assurances that her old bones could survive the strains of removal, the Admiralty agreed.

20,000 spectators lined docksides and quays when the big day came on October 13 – harbour officials anxiously watching the tide gauge. Two feet short of water, Unicorn was 50 minutes behind schedule when she got under way.

All went well, though – and Unicorn, launched at Chatham in 1824, now enjoys an active retirement, open to visitors as a valued survivor of ship construction in the immediate post-Napoleonic era. [*November 1962*]

35 *Tiger burns bright in the winter chill*

In the middle of January, when the United Kingdom was covered in a blanket of snow and ice in a notoriously severe winter, this photograph of HMS Tiger was received in the Navy News office. Amid waving palms, warmth and sunshine she wears the flag of the Flag Officer Second-in-Command Far East Fleet, saluting that of his superior on leaving Singapore in the December of the preceding year. [*February 1963*]

36

36 *Valentine for Oracle*

HMS Oracle, fifth of the Oberon and Porpoise hunter-killer class to be completed at the Cammell Laird shipyard at Birkenhead was commissioned on St Valentine's Day. [*March 1963*]

37 *Barrosa battles with pirates off Borneo*

To assist the Royal Navy's search for arms and ammunition smuggling round the coasts of Sarawak, Brunei and Sabah – formerly British North Borneo – the Sultan of Brunei provided specially built Peraus small craft which were easily manoeuvrable in the narrow channels between the mangrove swamps.

HMS Barrosa was acting as guardship in operations against Indonesian terrorists. Able Seaman Charles Sutherland died after a gun battle with pirates. He was one of a boarding party from the fleet radar picket which stopped a powered boat with 13 pirates on board. Three were captured immediately – but in an exchange of shots Sutherland was fatally wounded while the other ten jumped overboard. One was later sighted on land – seriously wounded

37

35

he died later, after saying he believed the rest had drowned.

For decades the pirates of the Sulu Sea SW of the Philippines had made the Borneo coast their happy hunting grounds. With the advent of the outboard motor they had been able to strike and disappear before the authorities could intervene. Ships of the Far East Fleet were often called upon to search for them – but they were able to steal up upon isolated villages, loot local shops, kill and steal boats and outboard engines and make a swift getaway long before a search could be organised. [*March 1963*]

40

38 **Peaceful invasion at Anzio**

After over a year in the Persian Gulf, the tank landing ship HMS Anzio was making her way home for a long refit when she made her first call at the Italian resort from which she took her name. Nineteen years earlier there had been little left of Anzio. The battle which followed the Allied landings had lasted many weeks – though the seaborne operation had been a complete success. In the first 22 hours 36,000 men and 3,000 vehicles were brought ashore, but once the Germans had recovered from the initial shock they held back the advance at the bridge depicted on the ship's crest. The destroyers Janus, Jervis and Inglefield and the cruisers Spartan and Penelope, together with many assault craft, were lost.

Now the Anzio's 115 ship's company found a neat and cheerful seaside town preparing for a peaceful invasion of summer visitors from Rome, 30 miles away. To mark her visit, a gold medal showing the Maid of Anzio, a statue found there in the Emperor Nero's villa, was presented by local dignitaries, the Welfare Committee made a donation to the Santa Maria Goretti orphanage, and a small party travelled to the Holy City for an audience with the Pope. [*May 1963*]

39 **Deep water berth for Protector**

HMS Protector, the Royal Navy's Ice Patrol Ship, comes alongside the ice shelf at the head of Laubeuf Fiord, Adelaide Island Antarctica. "...in the foreground is the harbour-master – Mr Penguin. With his back to the ship he may have been expressing his disgust at the intrusion, or maybe he was 'camera-conscious' and wished to show off his stiff shirt." The permanent ice shelf provided an unusually deep water berth – the ship's echo sounder recorded 1,400 ft. When she returned to Portsmouth on May 15 at the end of her eighth successive season in the Antarctic Protector was carrying the highest proportion of volunteers of any RN ship – many of whom asked to return on one of the Royal Navy's most unusual commissions. While investigating shallow water north of the desolate South Sandwich Islands Able Seaman Ronald Winmill noticed an uncharted and rapidly shoaling bottom. The change from an average depth of well over 1,000 ft to a reading of only 90ft was so sudden that Protector's engines were put astern immediately. A detailed examination next day showed that Winmill had discovered an underwater volcano, the rim of which could be clearly seen close under the surface. [*May 1963*]

39

38

40 *False sense of security in Sarawak*

Against this idyllic sylvan backdrop the mineseeper HMS Woolaston looks happily secure – but the jungle of Sarawak concealed an everpresent threat of terrorist attacks from neighbouring Indonesian Borneo. She was carrying supplies for the helicopters of 845 Squadron in the Belaga area. The Royal Marines, Gurkhas and local security forces were on constant patrol here, searching out and repelling the marauders, manning ambushes and guarding native villages against infiltration along the 700-mile border. In such territory success depended on airdrops of men and supplies – and the helicopters needed their own support. [*December 1963*]

41 *Trouble in Tanganyika*

On her way to the Far East HMS Centaur – seen here on departure from Portsmouth – was soon in the news. She was diverted to take part in the rescue of survivors from the cruise liner Lakonia and her helicopters also recovered 50 bodies from the blazing wreck and landed them at Gibraltar. Later she picked up 500 Royal Marine Commandos of 45 Cdo at Aden and sped off to help put down an insurrection in Tanganyika. At the request of President Nyerere they were airlifted to Dar-es-Salaam amid a diversionary barrage from the carrier and the destroyer HMS Cumbria. They stormed Colito Barracks and, after some shooting, between 600 and 700 Askaris fled into the bush. They then mounted guard in the city to protect strategic points.

• The other carrier in this picture is HMS Hermes. The frigates Murray and Wakeful are on the right with the cruiser Bermuda lying astern of Centaur. [*February 1964*]

42 *"If you bend it, we'll mend it"*

HMS Ausonia , then the oldest ship in the Royal Navy – apart from HMS Victory which remains in commission to this day – left Malta for the last time after six years service to the Mediterranean Fleet, for the last two years of which she had worn the flag of the Flag Officer Flotillas (Mediterranean).

The Grand Old Lady of Lazaretto Creek had carried out repairs to a lot of ships in that time, supplying them with vast quantities of steam, electricity and stores, servicing and repairing radar and radio sets, guns and control equipment, motors and generators overhauling engines, repairing – often rebuilding – hundreds of ship's boats, making awnings, splicing wires. All of which amply justified her demanding motto "Si Frangitus Reparamus – freely translated as "If you bend it, we'll mend it." Built 43 years before as a Cunard liner for the North Atlantic run, she was taken over by the Royal Navy in September 1939 and converted as an armed merchant cruiser.In this capacity she was employed in the Atlantic until 1941. In May 1942 she was converted finally as a heavy repair ship and saw service in the Far East. At the end of the war she went into reserve at Chatham, returning to duty after a refit at Devonport as repair ship of the Mediterranean Fleet in place of Ranpura in 1958.

42

41

With the run-down at Malta, Ausonia gradually took on extra duties, notably as submarine depot ship and with responsibility for the Msida Minesweeping Base on the departure of HMS Narvik in 1962. The departure of Ausonia marked the end of the 5th Submarine Division in Malta. It was the end of an era "studded with honour", the Flag Officer Submarines signalled her: "Submariners remember with affection their association with Malta, and the Malta Squadron, be it the 2nd, 1st, 10th or 5th, and with pride the duties performed by them in two world wars. They remember, too, the happy and willing help given to them by their depot ships, their shore support and indeed by the people of Malta itself." [*September 1964*]

43 **Grey ghost that haunted the Borneo coast**

"The 'Grey Ghost's' commission ends... HMS Albion was back in Portsmouth at the end of 18 months East of Suez. When the Brunei rebellion broke out in Northern Borneo she was heading east across the Indian Ocean for Singapore. Ordered to the trouble spot "with all dispatch" she set off on a 3,000 mile high speed dash. 40 Commando, which had been embarked at Aden, was airlifted ashore by the ship's two helicopter squadrons – 845 (Wessex) and 846 (Whirlwind) – to reinforce the troops already there. 846 was disembarked to be based at Brunei Airport while 845 operated from on board, flying troops ashore to cut off or surround rebel forces as intelligence reports or reconnaissance flights revealed their positions. At the same time the ship's four assault landing craft were detached to Brunei, where they were kept busy on river patrols and on logistic supply to units up-river.

When disastrous floods came – the worst in living memory – relief work became a top priority. Tons of food, fuel and oil, together with medical supplies, were flown to the floodstricken areas. Troops had to be evacuated and civilians, suffering from exposure and near-starvation were flown to reception areas where the Army and Government medical services could take over. Throughout, the weather was appalling and severely curtailed fixed-wing flying. The helicopters were not so restricted – they could creep up the river valleys or between the cloud and the jungle top and hover or land as required.

Although by April 1963 the emergency in Brunei was over and only a few hard-core rebels were at large, ominous reports were being received from Sarawak When armed men attacked the police station and armoury at Tebedu near the Indonesian border, 846 Sqn was rushed from Brunei to Kuching while Albion, with 845 Sqn embarked, sailed at short notice from Singapore with reinforcement troops to round up the rebel infiltrators and contain the threat from members of the clandestine communist organisation from within.

The underlying cause of the rebel activity both in Brunei and Sarawak was the impending formation of the new Federation of Malaysia which Indonesia opposed and intended to crush. Indonesia's 'confrontation' gathered momentum as the birth of Malaysia drew near. Eventually Brunei decided not to join the Federation, but on September 16, 1963 Malaysia – uniting Sarawak, Sabah (formerly North Borneo) with Malaya and Singapore – came into being together with a marked increase in rebel activity.

43

Both squadrons were heavily committed ashore while Albion flitted from Singapore to various parts of Northern Borneo carrying replacements or reinforcements of troops, stores and aircraft – fixed wing Pioneers, Austers and Beavers were embarked as well as Belvedere, Sycamore and Whirlwind helicopters.

Serious as the situation was in these parts, there were several potential trouble spots in East Africa and the Middle East, any of which might erupt and require Albion, the commando ship – but her squadrons were committed to Borneo.

Thus she started her 'secret mission' – a 12,000 mile high speed journey to Tobruk and back to fetch RAF Belvedere and Whirlwind Mk X helicopters so that the two naval air squadrons could be withdrawn from Borneo to return to a commando ship role.

But the arrival of 1964 saw more trouble posed by the Indonesian-based rebels – particularly in Sabah, an area which had previously been relatively quiet. So 845 and 846 were again landed ashore – the latter at Tawau with 845 in the Sibu area of Sarawak, 1,000 miles apart.

They had barely become established when the Zanzibar Government was overthrown, followed soon by mutinies by African troops in Tanganyika, Uganda and Kenya. British help was requested and it was not long before the signal was received "Albion is required in East Africa. Your Squadrons are to remain in Borneo."

Arriving in Mombasa on February 9, 45 Commando, units of the 16th/5th Lancers, 814 Sqn and two RAF Belvederes were transferred to Albion from HMS Victorious, which had withdrawn the troops from Tanganyika where the police role had been taken over by 1 Commando.

And so Albion became once more a commando ship – ready to land a fighting force at almost a moment's notice. Although an easing of the internal unrest in East Africa enabled the embarked troops to be landed at Aden, Albion remained on the Middle East Station until the end of her commission.

By then she had sailed 85,000 miles and her squadrons had flown 10,000 operational sorties. Because of her frequent appearances off the coast of Borneo, generally arriving at first light, "she assumed a phantom-like quality which led her to be known as 'the old grey ghost of the Borneo Coast'". [*May 1964*]

44

44 *Tanked up with helicopters*

The tank landing ship HMS Lofoten – first commissioned in 1945 and named in honour of the first successful Commando action of the Second World War – came out of Devonport Dockyard after extensive conversion to fit her in her new role as the Royal Navy's first helicopter support ship. The upper deck was stripped and reinforced to form a flight deck and hangar facilities provided to house four helicopters, allowing them to operate at greater ranges from their main support base.

She is seen here just prior to conversion with a "rougher-up" strip on the deck used for trials. *[July 1964]*

45

45 *Death of a Naval hero*

A Naval escort draws Sir Winston Churchill's bier through the streets of London. The great statesman had been First Lord of the Admiralty on two momentous occasions – at the beginning of both world wars. When he resigned after the failure of the Dardanelles expedition Kitchener had told him: "There's one thing they cannot take from you – the Fleet was ready." A quarter of a century later, when the unwelcome prophecies he made during his period in "the wilderness" of political disfavour had proved only too true, the Board signalled the Navy: "Winston is back". Both statements suggest a deeper understanding of maritime strategy and a more intimate sensitivity for the needs of the Senior Service than modern historians are prepared to credit him with – but the Navy News editorial on his passing was unequivocal: "Sir Winston loved, and, what is more to the point, *understood* the Royal Navy, its functions as "Britain's Sure Shield", its needs, its difficulties, its potentialities, and he knew its officers and men. He knew, in both wars, the tasks which faced the Navy and those difficult decisions he had to make, both as First Lord and as Prime Minister, he was able to make because of his complete understanding of the role and the men of the Navy, knowing that his demands would be met if it was within the power of men to do so.

"Winston Churchill knew the Navy when it was the largest in the world and he also knew it during – to use his own phrase – its finest hour: when it was stretched to its limits – aye, and beyond. But he did not hesitate to make hazardous calls upon it.That was the measure of his understanding – his trust in those who sailed the seas for Britain and their trust in him.

"Sir Winston Churchill is dead but the Royal Navy will always remember him. He takes his place with all the other naval heroes – Nelson, Blake, Collingwood, Drake, Rodney and so many others." *[February 1965]*

46 *Chocolate was Nigger's dark secret*

"In 1951 a large stray black dog wandered into HMAS Penguin in Sydney, Australia, and was adopted by the Fourth Submarine Division of the Royal Navy. He was christened 'Nigger' and over the course of time became the mascot of the squadron. "Nigger remained with the Division and was cared for entirely by the ship's company, including his Veterinary fees, an item never insignificant in his early fighting days and again latterly as he grew older. With unfailing regularity Nigger saw every submarine off to sea and again on return to harbour, boarded any transport with submarine ratings in it and kept HMAS Penguin clear of lesser dogs.

"Unfortunately Nigger was involved in a road accident on January 11, 1965, and died the next day as a result of his injuries.

"His early days were full of energy

and vigour, he has been known on many occasions to leave Penguin at the same time as the bus to Neutral Bay, a distance of seven miles from the depot, and no matter how hard the bus driver tried, Nigger would always be on the jetty before the bus arrived. He took an active part in all sports. He was a good swimmer and a great footballer (as many a league referee found to his confusion). He would run after the ball and if by chance took hold of the lacing it was a long and hard chase that followed.

"Nigger's aquatic ability was outstanding, he would nudge anyone he fancied into the pool and stroke for stroke the race was on.

"His interests were wide and varied. He didn't like alcohol but when in the Wet Canteen did his utmost to bolster the profits of a well-known chocolate firm. Even if the beer didn't interest him the sing-songs were right up his street and he joined in lustily. Like a true submariner he roamed the depot looking for WRANS who were all fond admirers of his.

"He would spend hours chasing seagulls up and down the jetty with nothing to show for it at the end. His runs ashore varied from Sunday dinner at home with someone on Ration Allowance; an afternoon on Plonk Island off Balmoral Beach, to a really good run on a Saturday night to the Manly Hotel with the lads. One particular Saturday the manager asked for Nigger to be removed. The lads moved instead and had a better run in the Pacific Hotel, the Manly taking less that evening than for a long time. One outstanding feature that separated him from other submariners was that he was tidy. When he had finished his fish and chip supper he would screw up the remains in the paper and push it all into a corner of the mess deck and then look round waiting for the applause.

"Despite the fact that Nigger loved salt water he hated fresh and it would take some considerable effort by three or four stalwarts to drag him into the bathroom for a wash.

"Many submariners past and present from HM Submarines Telemachus, Thorough, Tactician, Andrew, Aurochs, Anchorite, Tapir, Tabard, Tactiturn and Trump will remember his antics and companionship around the depot, on his Sunday morning walks and on the front row seat he always occupied in the Penguin Cinema.

"Nigger meant a lot to the Fourth Submarine Division and he will be sadly missed by all those in the Submarine Service and the Royal Australian Navy who knew him. It is hoped that eventually he will be put in a place of honour in the Submarine Museum in HMS Dolphin as a lasting tribute to his faithfulness."

(Eventually he was – and there Nigger's mortal remains, having submitted to the taxidermist's art, remain, sadly very far from home. The author of this touching portrait of one of the Submarine Service's indelible personalities may be forgiven if he did not determine the subject's own preference for their disposal). [*March 1965*]

46

47

47 Brereton bags Belgian poachers

HMS Brereton, a 'Ton' class coastal minesweeper serving with the Fishery Protection Squadron and seen here off St Michael's Mount, Cornwall, arrested three Belgian trawlers fishing within the 12 mile limits off the coast of North Wales.The Milford Haven Fishery Inspector had indicated that large numbers of 'poachers' were putting the local fishermen out of business. The 'Battle of Liverpool Bay" unfolded as Brereton, suitably disguised, arrived under cover of darkness off Great Ormes Head...

"Belgian trawlers are invariably of steel construction, as opposed to many of the local boats fishing in the area which are made of wood. Consequently the first large juicy radar contact, at almost eight miles from the shore, was selected. The ship was within two cables of this contact before the disguise was lifted, the Gemini dinghy lowered and the first boarding party directed to the trawler to investigate his suspected unlawful business. The trawler was Belgian with several baskets of live fish on the upper deck, and he had clearly recently hauled his trawl....

"Some ten minutes later a second boarding party was sent away to investigate another Belgian trawler, which was actually fishing 8.7 miles from the nearest land, and finally a third boarding party was directed to a third vessel which was caught shortly before he had recovered his gear at 10 miles from the shore. The reminder of the Belgian fleet were steaming at maximum revolutions for the 12-mile limit

"Having detached the three boarding parties, each consisting of one officer and three or four ratings, the ship left the scene to take the names and numbers of those vessels which

were more fortunate and had fled across the border when they had received the alarm on their R/T sets."

Later, Brereton and the three trawlers proceeded to Birkenhead where each skipper was fined £250, plus costs and his gear confiscated. With the loss of five days fishing time, the penalties were probably over £1,200 for each vessel – then the highest awarded to any foreign fishing vessel caught poaching in the waters of the British Isles. Never before had so many been caught collectively breaking the law. [*August 1965*]

48 *Less bovver with a hovver*

The latest phase in an extensive series of Far East trials of the SRN 5 hovercraft took place on the rapids of the twisting jungle rivers Rajang and Batang Bului in Malaysian Borneo. Here one of the two hovercraft – operated by a joint Navy/Army team – negotiates the narrow and dangerous stretch near Sibu. During the trials 112 miles were covered in 2½ hours. [*December 1965*]

49 *Four for all*

The Dartmouth Training Squadron comprised four Whitby Class frigates – Tenby, Torquay, Scarborough and Eastbourne (pictured here). Its main task was to provide basic ship experience for officer cadets. It also offered sea time for young Royal Marines officers and Engine Room Artificer apprentices. [*February 1966*]

50

50 *Cannonade for the full wax*

When Madame Tussaud's began constructing the tableau of the Battle of Trafalgar that would become one of the famous London waxworks museum's star attractions, they wanted the sound effects to be as realistic as possible. Lieut. Douglas Denyer and CPO Robert Bamber, from the gunnery school at HMS Excellent, prepared to fire one of the original guns carried by Nelson's flagship HMS Victory. The ancient cannon's flintlock – an innovation that in 1805 helped give the edge over the combined French and Spanish fleet – was primed and an authentic powder charge combined with a paper ball rammed into the barrel. After the first thunderclap boom had rolled around the historic Portsmouth Dockyard, the sound engineers asked for a repeat – and the pair duly obliged, to the delight of the watching crowd. The cannonade was eventually combined with the din of shouted orders and the yells and screams of seamen, feverishly bringing their guns to bear in the close confines of the gundecks as the enemy's returning fire blasted lethal spinters of oak into them at point blank range. No wonder many of the survivors were deafened for life... [*September 1966*]

48

49

51

51 *Link-up at Leningrad*

Smiling Russian interpreter Olga links arms with A/B Harry Pursey as sailors from HMS Devonshire visit the summer palace of Czar Peter the Great at Petrodvoretz near Leningrad, now St. Petersburg. The guided missile destroyer was paying goodwill visits to Leningrad, Helsinki and Gdynia. [*November 1966*]

52 *Air strike on Torrey Canyon*

"The Fleet Air Arm is delighted with the success of bombing operations to fire the oil in the wreck of the tanker Torrey Canyon on Seven Stones Reef off Land's End."

Their satisfaction was summed up in the words of Lieut.-Cdr David Howard, commanding officer of 736 Sqn, who led the initial operation.

"We felt great. We are very pleased with the accuracy of the attack and are delighted the Fleet Air Arm was asked to do it, and did it in one afternoon."

The tanker had been aground for 11 days when the decision was reached to fire the remaining oil aboard. On March 28 Buccaneer jets flew from Lossiemouth and dropped 42 1,000lb bombs, quickly followed by RAF Hunter jets with drop cans of aviation fuel. Flames and smoke billowed into the sky. The other Fleet Air Arm squadron taking part was No 800 (Lieut.-Cdr James Moore). Seventy-five per cent of the bombs were on target, and both sections of the wreck had direct hits.

Mr Foley, Under-Secretary for Defence (Navy), sent the following message: 'Splendid show.Well done. Congratulations all round.'

"Exceptionally high tides extinguished the blaze and there were renewed attacks on following days, bringing a wartime atmosphere in the southwest... Sea Vixens from Yeovilton and Buccaneers from Brawdy as well as more RAF Hunters with napalm joined in until the wreck was declared to be free from oil.

"Less spectacular were the surface operations which continued from the time the tanker went aground and mounted in scale and importance as the oil drifted ashore. Warships which have been mentioned included Barrosa Delight, Aurora, Daring, Eskimo, Carysfort and Blackwood and the minesweepers Clarveston, Wotton and Nurton. Another task force for Channel Islands operations consisted of Pellew, Laleston, Belton Highburton and Soberton."

• Smoke shrouds the flames rising from the blazing Torrey Canyon, the most notorious pollution disaster to assail home waters in the post war era. First direct hits were scored by Lieut.-Cdr D Mears, senior pilot of 800 Sqn, and his observer, Lieut Reardon. [*April 1967*]

53

53 *Last calls for tragic star Jayne*

When HMS Monkton visited Newcastle-upon-Tyne, film star Jayne Mansfield was welcomed on board at the invitation of the midshipmen. Shortly after this photograph was taken the only 'dumb blonde' icon of the Fifties and Sixties to rival Marilyn Monroe in popular memory was decapitated in a motor accident. [*May 1967*]

54 *Flypast over Aden*

Aircraft from the carriers HMS Victorious and Hermes fly in formation over the Aden State and Al Ittihad – on the eve of a new Middle East crisis.

Admiral Sir John Hamilton was hauling down his flag as Commander-in-Chief Mediterranean, marking the virtual end of British seapower in the 'Middle Sea' – command of all Royal Navy ships in the Mediterranean would pass to the C-in-C, Home Fleet. [*June 1967*]

52

55 **Fresh sightings on Socotra**

An unusual voyage was undertaken by the 360-ton minesweeper HMS Appleton to the sparsely populated island of Socotra in the Indian Ocean and the neighbouring islands of Abdal Kuri and Darsa Sumdra. Sixteen scientists were embarked to carry out a full-scale geological, entomological, botanical, archaeological and linguistic survey – and a RAF opthalmic surgeon who was able to restore the sight of 16 Socotrians.Abdal Kuri had not been visited by a Royal Navy ship since HMS Penzance in 1933 and navigation was often difficult due to the inaccuracy of the Socotra chart, compiled in 1835 and still the only one in use. [*July 1967*]

55

56 **On camera in Canada**

HMS Hampshire and HMS Euryalus pass under the Jacques-Cartier Bridge at Montreal while visiting Canada's hugely acclaimed Expo 67.

57

The Hampshire's reception at Toronto included a firefloat welcome pictured against the background of the city's skyscrapers. [*August 1967*]

54

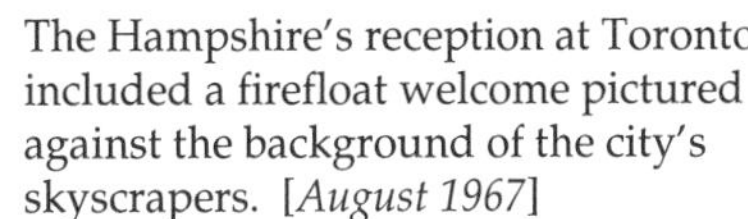

56

58a

58b

59

58 *Princess of style – Royal fashion at Fulmar*

"A study in hemlines" as Princess Margaret enters the Wrens' block at HMS Fulmar, the RN air station at Lossiemouth, opening new living quarters for more than 1,000 naval personnel.

Fashion commentary in Navy News in those days was wearily stilted and warily self-conscious – yet no royal visitor wore Sixties styles with more panache.

• The visit over, Captain D G Parker makes plain his appreciation of the Countess of Snowdon's boa-feathered polka dot ensemble.
[*September 1967*]

59 *Timely Resolution*

HMS Resolution, the Royal Navy's first Polaris submarine, commissioned at Barrow-in-Furness on October 2 – right on time.Armed with 16 A-3 Polaris missiles with British warheads capable of being delivered with extreme accuracy at a range of 2,500 miles, she could operate all over the world without the need to surface and presented "almost insuperable problems of detection to an enemy," providing a nuclear shield for Britain and NATO. Here, at speed on the surface, she shows the unusual wave formation built up at her whale-like bow. She would join the Fleet the following year after tests at Cape Kennedy. [*October 1967*]

60 **Warspite in the wet**

When HMS Warspite, the Royal Navy's third nuclear-powered submarine, arrived at Singapore, the oriental parasols carried by the waiting wives were used as a protection against the monsoon rain. Warspite was the third RN 'nuke' to visit the Far East in the past year. The day before her arrival, her commanding officer, Cdr Robert 'Tubby' Squires – who would become Flag Officer Submarines in the late 70s – learned by radio that he had been selected for promotion to Captain the following June. [*February 1968*]

60

61 **Polaris made perfect**

'Perfect in every respect! was the report when a Polaris missile was launched from HMS Resolution – the first from a British submarine. Resolution was cruising submerged about 30 miles off Cape Kennedy, Florida, when she hurled the weapon to the target area down the Atlantic Missile Test Range. Watchers from the attendant vessels saw a swirl of green water. Seconds later the missile burst through the surface in a fountain of foam. The firing was carried out by the Port Crew, under Cdr Michael Henry. -watched by Vice-Admiral Sir Hugh Mackenzie, Chief Polaris Executive, who radioed: "The event is the culmination of a great effort on the part of the submarine commanding officer and his crew, and by the British shipyards, firms and technicians who have built and tested the submarine and its systems.

"It has also set one more example of the efficiency of the Polaris weapons system, which was designed, developed and perfected in the United States of America." [*March 1968*]

61

62 **Brains and brawn before beauty**

The first three Phantoms for the Royal Navy – the F4K navy version arrived at the RN Air Station from the United States, having staged via Newfoundland and the Azores. They are seen here escorted by a Sea Vixen from 892 Squadron. With its "dejected-looking downswept tail arrangement" the Phantom was said to be no beauty – but its impending arrival had sustained the Fleet Air Arm through the shocks of recent defence reviews and "the still unbelievable decision to phase out carriers and fixed-wing capability".

When they first appeared nine years earlier, the Phantoms marked a great leap forward, with a speed almost twice that of sound. Succeeding models had achieved seven world speed records and the Royal Navy Phantoms had Rolls Royce Spey engines providing extra static thrust for short take-offs and rapid climb compared with the American Navy type.

62

This was not the only British contribution to the interceptor fighter aircraft that was by now formidably outstanding in the world's air forces. In all, nearly half the components were British, including the Martin-Baker escape system, entirely automatic and of proven reliability in Service use. A major item of electronic equipment was a high-powered, forward-looking radar and missile computer system to serve Sparrow and Sidewinder missiles for air-to-air attack.

The Phantom would be able to carry more than eight tons of external payload – conventional or nuclear bombs, fuel tanks, air-to-ground missiles, rockets, mines, napalm and cannon – on five stations beneath the wings and fuselage. [*June 1968*]

63 Four walls do not a prison make

Boar hunting in Izmir provided a diversion for the bolder spirits among HMS Alcide's ship's company during a two month sojourn in the Mediterranean – where the bag included a cow that was being milked at the time...

On the way home from Piraeus to Malta a short cut was taken through the Corinth Canal – three miles long but only 80 ft wide, a tight fit even for a submarine.

The trip back from Gibraltar to Portsmouth was enlivened by the presence of an officer and six other ranks of the Queen's Own Hussars, who had hitched down to the Rock in HMS Naiad and failed to get a lift back with the RAF.

"Passing through the Bay of Biscay their Sergeant, a Pole who had spent part of the war in a Russian prison camp, announced that he wished he was back there!" [*August 1968*]

63

64

64 Marooned in the ice

On her first visit to the far south since taking over as the Royal Navy's ice patrol ship HMS Endurance helped rescue six stranded men from the British Antarctic Survey.

"We first heard that a Twin Otter of the BAS had force-landed on the almost inaccessible Larsen ice-shelf when we were approaching South Georgia, 1,000 miles away.

"Immediately, we turned in a rough sea and Force 9 gale, beginning the long haul down to the ice, and when we reached the pack ice deliberately began bashing through it. During the next 24 hours we penetrated the ice 75 miles and were close enough to fly off our two helicopters to Stonington, the BAS base about 100 miles south of the Antarctic Circle, and on the west coast of Grahamland.

"Bad weather and the fact that they

cannot fly in freezing cloud prevented crossing of the 5,000 ft Grahamland plateau to the position 45 miles east of Stonington which the fuel-less Twin Otter had reached.

"After five abortive attempts in four days, a weather break gave the aircrew the chance to reach the marooned plane... The men were in good heart, although they had survived on little more than cold spaghetti and meat and had only four sleeping bags between six." [*March 1969*]

65 *'Left a bit, right a bit...'*

Stars of the long-running BBC radio comedy series "The Navy Lark' Jon Pertwee and Leslie Phillips continue their long battle with the mysteries of navigation as HMS Troubridge pays her last visit to London. The Navy's oldest seagoing warship would shortly pay off off at Chatham after 27 years' service, following a busy last 12 months which took her to the Far East, Australia, South Africa and the Mediterranean. While in the capital, the Type 15 anti-submarine frigate paid her last respects to Walthamstow, whose Savings Committee had raised the £2m she cost to build back in 1942.

During her long career, HMS Troubridge steamed nearly 600,000 miles, 90,000 of them during her last commission. Originally built as a destroyer, she took part in many actions during World War II and in one operation spent 62 days continuously at sea. She was converted in 1957, acquiring a Leopard-type enclosed bridge and an additional deck to fit her for her new role.

Despite her association with the disaster-prone HMS Troutbridge of "Navy Lark" fame, she made it home for the last time without mishap. But generations of hapless young navigating officers are still suffering comparison with Sub-Lieutenant Phillips' legendary lack of any sense of direction. [*June 1969*]

66

66 *Blake lays out the carpet*

A Hawker Siddeley Harrier close support jet fighter landed on the flight deck of the command helicopter cruiser HMS Blake in trials to test the 'jump jet' vertical take-off plane's capability for operations from ships in the mid-1970s. The aircraft was flown from Dunsfold airfield in Surrey by Hawker Siddeley chief test pilot Hugh Merewether, to rendezvous with the Blake south east of the Isle of Wight.

Laid down in 1942, the Blake was not commissioned until 1961 – by which time her original design fit of nine six-inch guns and ten four inch turrets had been exchanged for two twin six inch and three twin three inch turrets. A 21-month commission followed, mostly spent carrying the flag of Flag Officer Flotillas Mediterranean. She then spent six years in Dockyard hands, her after superstructure and armament being replaced by facilities for an air group, comprising a flight deck and hangar for Sea King helicopters, with workshops, offices, briefing room and new cabins and mess decks below.

To create space for the air group, the gunnery branch suffered the loss of two twin three-inch and the aft twin six inch batteries – but were compensated by the siting of two quadruple Sea Cat missile launchers amidships.

Even so, the Blake went to sea with the largest guns in the Royal Navy –and if called upon to do so, remained capable of laying down a heavy carpet of shells. [*September 1969*]

65

67

67 *Portland arena for Dark Gladiator*

Showing her paces here was the smallest fighting unit of the Fleet – HMS Dark Gladiator.One of the two operational Dark Class fast patrol boats left in service, she ran out of Portland for the Flag Officer Sea Training. Her roles included acting as Search and Rescue night boat for HMS Osprey and occasionally as an Admiralty Underwater Weapons Establishment trials ship. Well over 12 years old, she could still manage a top speed of over 40 knots. [*December 1969*]

The 1970s

HERMES TO SAIL ON

Hundreds of men who were due to leave H.M.S. Hermes after she returned to Portsmouth this autumn to start refit will now be sailing on with her in the New Year.

A reshuffled dockyard programme, in which industrial action has played its part, has affected a number of vessels, including the Navy's largest ship. Present plans are for the carrier, which has a ship's company of about 1,000 including 900 ratings, to return in the spring in preparation for a May start on the refit, which will include the addition of a Harrier ski jump ramp.

When it became clear that the Hermes would be spending extra months at sea, a drafting officer from H.M.S. Centurion visited her at Norfolk, Virginia, in September with drafting proposals covering the additional sea time.

About 150 ratings expecting to come ashore on completion of their current sea service have had their spell in the ship extended, including 65 volunteers. Only about 20 men, however, will have to complete more than 30 months at sea (compared with normal sea time of 27 months). Importantly, additional sea service will "earn" shore time at an increased rate.

For many men due for "through draft" to other ships or to stay with the Hermes as she entered refit, the change of plan will mean more sea time in the carrier in early 1980.

Queries

On his visit to the Hermes, the drafting officer liaised with heads of Departments and departmental Regulators and he returned to H.M.S. Centurion with about 160 assorted queries to be dealt with. Of 33 men who expressed a strong wish to leave the ship, only five will have to stay.

The carrier also has about 30 Royal Marines, most of whom will continue to serve on board for the extra sea time, although some will be relieved on their normal dates.

It is understood that after returning this autumn and a further spell at sea, the Hermes will be back at sea in the New Year on a training cruise which will include the Caribbean, before starting refit.

SALUTE TO MOUNTBATTEN

Brilliant sunshine heightens the colour and pageantry — but the mood is sombre as a nation bids farewell to a great man. The flag-draped coffin of Admiral of the Fleet Earl Mountbatten of Burma arrives at Westminster Abbey, and — with head bowed and boots reversed in the stirrups — Lord Louis' charger Dolly takes final leave of her master. Salute to Mountbatten — Pages 23-26.

WELL BRED!

Seventh and last of the present Island class, H.M.S. Alderney, seen here on sea acceptance trials wearing the flag of Hall Russell Ltd., the Aberdeen shipbuilders, was due to commission on October 6.

With the comment, "What a herd," the Alderney points out that, in the wake of H.M. ships Jersey and Guernsey, she completes a trio of Channel Island breed names. And she goes on to mention that she has Lieut.-Cdr. Bull as commanding officer and Lieut.-Cdr. Metcalf as first lieutenant.

Unofficial motto of the ship: "Creme de la creme."

Fife makes history in hurricane disaster

A prime minister broadcast to his countrymen from a British warship during the Dominica disaster.

This possibly unique event occurred when, with all the island's communications down, H.M.S. Fife broadcast half-hourly public information and music to the stricken population of 75,000 after Hurricane David had struck.

"Director of broadcasting" for Radio Fife was the ship's chaplain, the Rev. Graham Williams, working with the ship's D.J.s and an interpreter.

For four days it was the only communication many islanders had with the authorities.

On behalf of the Dominican community in the U.K., Navy News has received a letter from Mr. Arden Shillingford (High Commissioner for the Commonwealth of Dominica) expressing "gratitude, thanks and appreciation to Captain Fry and his gallant crew who rendered so much valuable assistance to our folks in Dominica when the island was ravaged by the recent hurricane."

COURAGE

He goes on, "We are much indebted for the courage and selfless concern and determination which so characterised their action during the crisis."

The story, with pictures, of how the Fife helped after the disaster is told in Page Nine.

SHIPS ON SAFARI

Royal Navy ships were taking part in two major NATO exercises in late September and early October, one in the Atlantic involving a total of 70 vessels and the other in the Mediterranean.

Exercise Ocean Safari, being held over wide areas of the North Atlantic and the Norwegian Sea, is designed to demonstrate and improve NATO's capability to provide maritime support to Europe in time of crisis or war.

More than 17,000 men, 70 ships and 200 aircraft from eight NATO nations are participating. A multi-national anti-submarine task group headed by Rear-Admiral P. G. M. Herbert, flying his flag in H.M.S. Hermes, and NATO's two Standing Naval Forces — Atlantic and Channel — are among ships involved.

For the major NATO annual exercise Display Determination, being held in the Med., five nations, including the U.K., will provide ships. This is designed to demonstrate NATO capability to reinforce and re-supply its Southern Region.

68 *On the eastern seabed*

Seven members of the Far East Fleet clearance diving team, led by Lieut.-Cdr Brian Braidwood, flew to Gan Island for diving and demolition training. Here two of them are inspecting the propeller of the wreck of the 16,000 ton tanker British Loyalty, torpedoed by a Japanese submarine in World War II [*February 1970*]

68

69 *Mod gear for snowmen*

"Looking a little like the first Britisher aiming to be on the moon, this Royal Marine models the 'mod gear' for Britain's 'snow Marines', to the apparent indifference of at least two familiar onlookers in London..." [*February 1970*]

69

70 *Crumpets for the Lion of Judah*

HMS Chichester gets a royal salute from Emperor Haile Selassie as she steams past his yacht Ethiopia during her triumphant visit to the Imperial Ethiopian Navy's annual Navy Days.

In the swimming, water polo, track and field sports, the Chichester had the best record of all visiting ships, and came second only to the Ethiopian Navy. She had two encounters with the Russian Navy, winning the tug-of-war and sustaining a hard-fought 1 – 1 draw at soccer.

The ship provided a guard of 36 to escort the colour at the graduation ceremony of cadets of the Imperial Ethiopian Naval College. When the Chichester received the 'Lion of Judah' with a Royal Salute and Royal Guard, he met officers and ratings and was entertained to tea of crumpets and strawberry jam – a traditional gesture from the Royal Navy to the 79-year-old Emperor, who had spent the years of the Italian occupation (1936-41) in England and would be deposed four years later. in 1974 [*April 1970*]

70

71 *Helo long-hop*

Flying over Land's End at the start of a record trip to John o' Groats is Fleet Air Arm Sea King helicopter No 587 from RN air station Culdrose.

It made the non-stop 'long-hop' flight of 602.95 miles in 4 hours 19 minutes 21 seconds – an 'observed performance' by the Royal Aeronautical Society.

No Service helicopter had attempted a non-stop flight of this distance before and the object was to prove the capabilities of the aircraft with long-range tanks fitted and the accuracy of its navigation system.

The Sea King came from 700 'S' Squadron, piloted by its CO, Lieut.-Cdr Victor Sirett. [*June 1970*]

71

72 **Windsors in Yarmouth**

He was the Royal Navy's senior Admiral of the Fleet – but the informal style he always preferred characterised the Duke of Windsor's visit to HMS Yarmouth when she called at Naples.

The Duke and his Duchess were passengers in a cruise liner when he was invited on board the Rothesay class anti-submarine frigate to renew an association with the Senior Service that dated back over 60 years.

He had entered the Naval College at Osborne in 1907, moved on to Dartmouth and served as a Midshipman in the battleship HMS Hindustan in the autumn of 1911, shortly after his investiture as Prince of Wales. King George V then ordained – to his son's great distress – that his education should continue at Oxford and in the Army and his naval career was over. But a month before his Abdication as King Edward VIII he spent two days with the Home Fleet at Portland, where according to First Lord of the Admiralty Sir Samuel Hoare he had the chance to display what would be practically the last public show of the famous charm that won millions of hearts in the 1920s, when he had been the 'Ambassador of Empire' – a role in which the Royal Navy also had its heyday:

"I had a unique opportunity of seeing the most attractive side of his personality. If, on the one hand. he was, as many thought, wayward and irresponsible, on the other hand, no-one could deny his surpassing talent for inspiring enthusiasm and managing great crowds. He seemed to know personally every officer and seaman in the Fleet. On one of the evenings there was a smoking concert in the aircraft carrier Courageous... The vast underdeck was packed with thousands of seamen. In my long experience of mass meetings I never saw one so dominated by a single personality. At one point he turned to me and said:'I am going to see what is happening at the other end.' Elbowing his way through the crowd, he walked to the end of the hall and started community singing to the accompaniment of a seaman's mouth organ. When he returned to the platform he made an impromptu speech that brought the house down.... There followed an unforgettable scene of the wildest and most spontaneous enthusiasm. Here, indeed, was the Prince Charming, who could win the hearts of all sorts and conditions of men and women and send a thrill through great crowds."

In this month of August 1970 the Queen allowed that he might be interred alongside his wife at the royal burial ground at Frogmore. After his death on May 28, 1972, the Duchess of Windsor flew from Paris for his funeral to be met at Heathrow by Admiral of the Fleet Earl Mountbatten, who had accompanied her husband on two of his Empire tours and was his naval ADC. The Duke's wishes were fulfiled when his widow joined him 14 years later.

72b

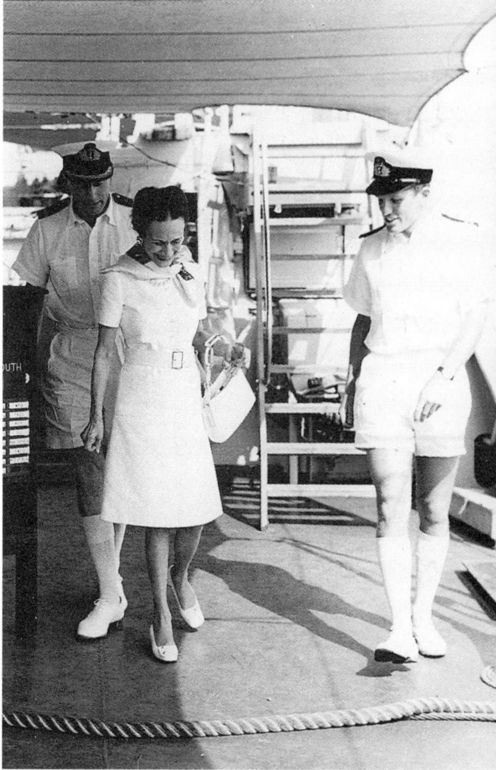

• The Duchess of Windsor laughingly observes a threat to her safe passage on board HMS Yarmouth, gallantly indicated by Lieut. R C Moore. In the previous year a television interview with Kenneth Harris had introduced her to the British public – over 11m viewers, three times the Tuesday Documentary's average audience – for the first time. [*August 1970*]

72a

73a

73b

73c

• Left to right: LME Harry Loader, AB Mick Leighton, CEM Mick Walsh, Mne Mick O'Rourke, ME Jock Lindsay, Mne Red Barell, Mne Henry Harris and AB Henry Hepworth glumly propose a last toast on HMS Victory's middle gun deck.

• Over the stern of the carrier HMS Albion goes the last of the 'gash' –tradition ordaining that the dregs of the rum tub must be 'ditched'. Stores Assistant Andrew Stevenson performs the office.

• More elaborate obsequies at HMS Dolphin, home of the Submarine Service.

73 'Dry Ginger' stops the tot

More tears were shed over the passing of the tot on 31 July than fell on the bier of Nelson.

Much of the outpouring of grief that attended the Admiralty's decision to do away with the rum issue was clearly tongue-in-cheek, though. By 1970 the daily award of an eighth of a pint of 95.5 proof spirit to every man in the Fleet had long been an anachronism – in a highly technical and sophisticated Navy no margin of error due to intoxication could be allowed and the era of harsh discipline, dire rations and living conditions scarcely fit for livestock in which rum had made life bearable was ancient history.

But over 300 years of tradition could not be allowed to end without due ceremony. In the Persian Gulf a rum barrel was buried with a headstone to mark the last resting place of a "good and faithful servant". Aboard HMS Dido, off the NE coast of Scotland, the last tot was thrown over the side in a sealed bottle – with instructions inside asking the finder to drink the Navy's health. The Alma Mater of the Submarine Service at HMS Dolphin, Gosport, provided a gun carriage bearing a coffin flanked by two drummers led by a piper playing a lament. And at a mess table in Nelson's last flagship HMS Victory the final issue was sipped with proper solemnity.

"I am not expecting to rocket up to the Top of the Pops in the Navy on this," said First Sea Lord Admiral Sir Michael "Dry Ginger" Le Fanu. But he made it clear there had been "no political pressures – it is a naval judgment."

The fiery spirit was first unofficially introduced into the Navy in 1655, when a British Fleet under Admiral Penn captured Jamaica. Its long-keeping qualities led to it becoming official issue in 1731, when the daily ration was set at a half-pint. Nine years

later the Commander -in-Chief West Indies Station, Admiral Vernon, reported: "The pernicious custom of the seamen drinking their allowance of rum in drams, and often at once, is attended with many fatal effects to their morals as well as their health..." When Vernon ordered it mixed with water he gave great offence to the tars, and since they had nicknamed him 'Old Grog' after the grograin boat cloak he habitually wore on the quarter deck in rough weather, so they tagged his watered down rum 'grog'.

As the tradition developed, grog was issued from the rum tub to leading rates and below. Chief Petty Officers and Petty Officers received their 'tot' neat – without water – at 1100, an hour before the grog issue, mixed two to one. Rum in the Royal Navy soon acquired its own patois – "Sippers", a small taste from a friend's issue; "Gulpers", one big swallow from another's tot; "Sandy Bottoms", to see off whatever was left in a friend's mug; "Splice the Mainbrace", a double tot for a job well done, or an invitation on board for free drinks.

Now CPOs, POs and Senior NCOs of the Royal Marines would be allowed to buy commercial spirits in their bars on board ship – a privilege previously enjoyed only by officers – while junior ratings, no longer allowed spirits on board, had their allowance of beer increased to three cans a day. As a fiscal compensation for the end of the rum issue , a capital sum of £2.7m was paid into a new sailors' fund. [*September 1970*]

74 **Flood relief in East Pakistan**

HMS Intrepid was part of the naval force that helped in the relief operation to flood-stricken East Pakistan, where thousands of people were engulfed by a huge tidal wave. The major part of the aid programme was provided by Great Britain in the biggest effort of its kind since the Second World War. The assault ship was joined by the repair ship HMS Triumph, sailing for the Ganges delta from Singapore. HMS Hydra was diverted there to survey the channels and a logistics ship, the RFA Sir Galahad, completed the Royal Navy's side of the tri-Service effort.

Skynet, the military satellite hanging in space 23,000 miles above the Indian Ocean which had been launched from Cape Kennedy in November 1969, received its biggest operational workout to date as it kept communication links between the British flotilla, the Singapore base and Whitehall. One of the system's terminals was located in the Intrepid, which played a vital part in co-ordinating the mercy mission.

Captain Tom Tayler, RM, who helped in the airlift of supplies, reported from the scene of the disaster:

"At a hundred feet the stench of death was unforgettable. Huddled in little groups, always close to a red flag which showed help was needed, the survivors waited anxiously for food and water. Our pilot wisely landed away from the pathetic groups, as only two days before starving islanders had jumped up at an American Bell helicopter and pulled it out of the sky. Three people were injured as the helicopter crashed to the ground.

"Within seconds of landing, the crowds reached us and, despite the efforts of the Royal Marine Commandos to keep them back, they quickly ripped open the sacks of rice and many of them began to eat it raw.

"Later, when I had time to talk to some of the people, I learned that on this particular island only 2,000 people survived out of an original 12,000. Most, I was told, had been swept out to sea. I saw no women or children under the age of seven. Only a few palm trees remained standing, and on one of them I was shown a water mark which was fully 15 feet from the ground...

"When the fleet arrived in the Bay of Bengal, the ships had to anchor 30 miles from the nearest land, owing to the silt in the bay caused by the cyclone. This fact alone stretched the communications and delivery of supplies to tremendous proportions. Navy helicopters flew up to 16 hours a day, while the landing craft flogged backwards and forwards ferrying thousands of tons of supplies into four major distribution points.

"As the rescuers navigated their small boats up the muddy rivers, they were able to see for themselves the horrific aftermath left by such a disaster. Few will ever forget the experience. It is likely to be many months before all the bodies are found and buried. No-one will ever know how many people died. Heavily populated as it is, this must be one of the most desolate and tragic areas of the world.It has taken this fantastic disaster to focus attention on its desperate plight." [*January 1971*]

74

75 Malacca Strait re-mapped

The hydrographic survey ship HMS Hydra in the Malacca Strait off Puala Undan. With existing charts no longer adequate for the increasing volume of super tankers and other deep draught shipping using the Strait, she was there to survey a 180-mile continuous channel ten miles wide. By January two thirds of the work had been done – with 70 shoals and three wrecks discovered.

The Hydra was fitted with echo sounders which provided a continuous profile of the seabed as she ran a closely spaced pattern of lines across the area. To be sure that no pinnacles of rock or wrecks were missed, contacts picked up on sonar sweeps were closely investigated.

The ship's position was fixed by an electronic system called Hi-Fix, using two radio stations ashore which leapfrogged down the coast in steps of about 40 miles to keep pace with the work.

Some work in the channel had previously been done by HMS Dampier, which surveyed in Malaysian waters for many years. [*March 1971*]

75

76 Dreadnought on top of the world

The nuclear Fleet submarine HMS Dreadnought pops up at the North Pole - the first British sub to do so.

Her patrol took her 1,500 miles under the ice before surfacing at the Pole, where a seaman with a rifle kept watch for prowling polar bears as other crew members ventured onto the ice cap. The Dreadnought had already broken through the ice three times on the way.

Describing her arrival at 8 a.m. on March 3, Lieut.-Cdr John Collier, torpedo and anti-submarine officer, said: "It was semi-twilight all the time and we spent several hours finding a suitable area of thin ice. We came to the surface through about a foot of ice at 5.30 in the evening and remained on the surface until the early hours of the morning.

"When you were out on the ice you had to make sure you didn't go too far from the submarine because it was an extremely hostile environment."

This was born out by the experience of LA(Phot) Michael Rowsell, who took this photograph soon after the submarine's 'fin' burst through. He had to operate his 35mm camera in 67 degrees of frost – but suffered a severe wind chill effect standing in a 20 knot draught filled with suspended ice crystals. Thus the fingers which just managed to press the shutter were numbed by a wind chill effect that plummeted to –110 degrees F.

HMS Dreadnought, commanded by Cdr Alan Kennedy, returned to the Clyde submarine base at Faslane on March 11. [*April 1971*]

76

77a

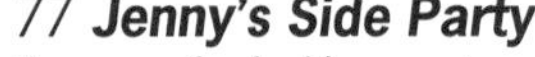

77 Jenny's Side Party

For nearly half a century one of the best-known and most popular figures around HMS Tamar had been the motherly Jenny, matriarch of the all-female side parties responsible for painting Hong Kong-based and visiting HM ships since 1928. Jenny and her famous side party spent a day on board the Leander-class frigate, HMS Danae, following an invitation from Captain R.S. McCrum, who was amazed to learn that Jenny had not

been to sea in anything larger than a sampan since 1960 when she sailed on board the cruiser Belfast.

With her team of cheerful and hardworking girls, Jenny had kept the Fleet shipshape for longer than most sailors could could remember. She had become a legend in her lifetime. Whenever a ship of the Royal Navy visited Hong Kong, Jenny and her side party descended on it and worked right through the ship's stay until the sides were spotless and the decks gleaming.

Jenny was virtually a member of the Royal Navy – she 'joined' in 1928 and her 'first ship' was the Berwick – with a Service Certificate that any Chief Boatswain's Mate would be proud of. Her string of 'VG Superiors' and (in the last couple of years) 'VG Exceptional's' were countersigned by Captains and Admirals.

Had the Navy changed in Jenny's forty-three years' service? "Not much ships still need painting," she said.

• *Left:* With appropriate headgear, Jenny sits in the Captain's seat on the Bridge of HMS Danae. Her escort is the ship's Public Relations Officer, Lt. Ian McClure.

• *Right:* Her team are also seen freshening up the carrier HMS Centaur. [*November 1971*]

77b

78 **Singapore in style**

Less fashionable than they once were, the elaborately posed, formal photographs of ship's companies popular in the days of Empire still have a unique appeal – if clothes make the man, it is her people that make a ship what she is. Here the anti-submarine frigate HMS Jaguar is "all present and correct" at Singapore. One of the first to serve there with the ANZUK force, she was soon scheduled to leave for Hong Kong. [*January 1972*]

78

79

81

79 *Campus Queen's dramatic end*

Lieut.-Cdr Mike Bracelin, commanding officer of HMS Beachampton, took this dramatic picture of the death throes of the former Cunard liner 'Queen Elizabeth' at Hong Kong, swept by fire from stem to stern.

Renamed 'Seawise University', the 83,000 ton Queen was within five days of sea trials following a £2m refit when plans to turn her into a floating campus came to a sudden end. A workforce of more than 1,200 had been toiling to convert her to her new role since her arrival in the Crown Colony in July 1971, but within hours she was reduced to a burnt-out shell.

In the foreground is HMS Yarnton, serving with the Sixth Mine Countermeasures 'Dragon' Squadron. She was among several ships and helicopters sent to the rescue – but so fierce was the blaze that she was forced to stand off and watch the end of a grand old lady of the seas. [*February 1972*]

80 *Against cheap alternatives*

HMS Cutlass, Scimitar and Sabre demonstrate their speed and manoeuvrability off Portland. It was the first time the members of the 1st Fast Training Boat Squadron had been pictured together since the squadron's formation in 1970. Accompanying the boats is a Wasp helicopter of 829 Naval Air Squadron.

Powered by twin Proteus gas turbine engines that gave them a top speed of over 40 knots they were used to train HM ships in the art of countering fast patrol boats – the cheap but powerfully armed units then being acquired by many of the world's smaller navies. [*June 1972*]

81 *Laleston warms to Arctic village*

The help given by a small Norwegian village to 161 men after a British troopship sank 200 miles north of – the Arctic Circle in 1940 was commemorated when HMS Laleston presented a plaque thanking the people of Bleik on the island of Andoy for their efforts in caring for the survivors.

Originally a tourist ship, the SS Vandyck was being used to bring men home from Norway when she was sunk by German aircraft. German troops were already stationed on Andoy and eventually the ship's survivors became prisoners of war. The ship's bell was salvaged by one of the villagers and was now dedicated in a new church tower.

• HMS Laleston heads towards Andenes on Andoy – enjoying the magnificent fjord scenery in a heat wave with temperatures in the 70s, well north of the Arctic Circle. [*August 1972*]

82 *Aeneas's last trip to the underworld*

A modified badge adorned the recently-acquired SLAM (Submarine Launched Airflight Missile) equipment of HMS Aeneas when she paid off at Devonport after a 27-year career. Instead of a spear, the warrior featured in the boat's crest brandishes a missile while his shield had been adapted to incorporate the Vickers Shipbuilding logo. Aeneas had been on hire to Vickers to demonstrate the system to representatives of the Royal Navy and several overseas navies in a series of

80

trials at the Ministry of Defence ranges at Eskmeals and Aberporth. SLAM used the Blowpipe missile operated by the Army as a portable anti-aircraft weapon and was considered to give submarines a low-cost attack capability against helicopters. [*December 1972*]

83 **Narwhal namesakes meet**

Two submarines of the same name – one British and one American – had a family gathering for the first time at Rosyth. The Porpoise Class HMS Narwhal (background) and the nuclear-powered attack sub USS Narwhal, commissioned in 1969, got together for this rare picture when the former was in for base maintenance and the latter – at 4,500 tons by three times the "big brother" – was visiting as part of a programme of exercises and visits in European waters. [*May 1973*]

82

83

84 *Cod War close-up*

"'At close quarters' is a phrase with real meaning in the Cod War as the Royal Navy goes about its business of protecting our trawlermen from harassment. On the left, the Icelandic gunboat Aegir steams away from a British trawler and HMS Cleopatra."

As the fishery dispute with Iceland turned into a fairground dodgem contest, the frigate HMS Lincoln consoled herself with a monster fish and chip supper – halibut steaks cut from a 2001b specimen presented to the Ship's Company by the trawler support vessel Othello.

For the men on the spot it all seemed much more serious: "In the battle of wills with the gunboats, the ops room have to be on their toes to sort out the gunboats from the jumble of some 30 trawlers and escorts. The radar screen often appears to have measles, and the Wasp helicopters are of great value in searching the area and identifying the various contacts.

"So the job continues... silence, searching, a sudden flurry of activity, then back again to cat-and-mouse. Danger is never far away, and it is indeed remarkable, having regard to the tactics involved, that nobody gets hurt... " [*July 1973*]

84

85 *Traffic jam at Tamar*

Three visiting Royal Navy ships, an Australian frigate and six Malay vessels joined ships of the Hong Kong Squadron to give HMS Tamar a real basinful of hardware.

Taking part in a world training cruise, the RN task force was headed by the command helicopter cruiser HMS Tiger, with the frigates HMS Rhyl and HMAS Yarra. The nuclear-powered submarine HMS Dreadnought put in her first appearance in Hong Kong and the RFAs Regent, Tidespring and Tidereach completed the largest 'fleet' seen there in recent years. [*October 1973*]

86 *Yes, we have no bananas*

The guided missile destroyer HMS Norfolk (top right) and frigates Leander and Achilles went to the aid of the Lebanese-registered Barrad Crest, on fire 20 miles east of Start Point.

While the 1,583 ton Barrad Crest was en route from Surinam with a cargo of bananas, fire started in the engine room and took hold of the after end of the ship.

Fire-fighting operations continued throughout the night until the Norfolk

85

was able to take her in tow, making six knots towards Plymouth through poor visibility, blinding rain and six-foot waves. When the tow was taken over by the PAS tugs Superman and Advice, an explosion blew off a hatch and injured seven firemen, the captain and and one crew member and a member of the PAS mooring party. The ship was beached while the casualties were removed to RN Hospital Stonehouse and the battle to contain the blaze continued over the weekend before pumping out could begin, two holds being filled with a pulpy mixture of sea water, burnt cardboard and soggy, burnt bananas... Five days later the Barrad Crest was pulled off the beach at Jennycliffe and put at a buoy. [*November 1973*]

87 **Dido, queen of the opera**

HMS Dido was at Sydney when The Queen opened the Opera House that would become the Australian city's most famous landmark – next to the Harbour Bridge, of course....

The ship later took part in joint exercises with the RAN on passage to Fremantle. [*December 1973*]

86

87

88

88 White South to Green Mansions

As HMS Endurance steams through the Patagonian Canals in Southern Chile en route to Valparaiso, the narrow channels, numerous waterfalls and dense rain forest make a welcome change from the treeless scenery of the Falklands and South Georgia – even the spectacular wild white wastes of Antarctica eventually leave the Navy's ice patrol ship longing for green places again.... [*March 1974*]

89 Norfolk's missile broadside

HMS Norfolk was the first British warship to fire the French Exocet sea-skimming missile – notoriously the scourge of the Task Force in the Falklands eight years later – and the destroyer was also the first RN ship to be fitted with three missile systems, Seaslug and Seacat making up the rest of her primary offensive capability. The successful evaluation trials were held in the Mediterranean off Toulon. [*June 1974*]

89a 89b

90 Morning in Moskva

0600 hours in the South Aegean Sea. Two hundred energetic sailors in shorts and track suits throng the flight deck for PT exercises – on board the Soviet helicopter carrier Moskva, at anchor in company with the Kara Class missile cruiser Nikolaev.

The scene was photographed from HMS Fearless, then the Dartmouth Training Ship, during her Mediterranean exercises. Her own early morning 'jerks' started half an hour later... [*August 1974*]

91 The light that failed

A Sea King helicopter from HMS Tiger lowers Lieut.-Cdr Ben Chilcott onto a narrow ledge beneath the navigational light beacon on Rockall, 200 miles into the Atlantic west of the Hebrides – the lonely rock pillar famous for its prominence in weather forecasts.

The beacon, installed in 1972 as part of Britain's claim to the area's territorial rights which had assumed greater significance as oil exploration and the fishing industry expanded, had failed after being pounded by heavy seas the previous October – and the Tiger was the first ship to pass by her with more than one helicopter embarked (necessary for safety) and with enough technical expertise to carry out running repairs.

In ideal weather – rare for Rockall – the landing party found the light's batteries heavily corroded and decided to remove the lantern assembly.They left behind a photograph of the ship and their names attached to the inside of the beacon's lid. During the operation one of HMS Tiger's helicopters carried out a quick trade with a friendly trawler and in exchange for a bottle of whisky returned with 3501b of fresh fish and two enormous halibut. [*September 1974*]

91

90

92 **Passing lightly over a 1,000 year problem**

Water ski-ing on the Suez Canal alongside HMS Maxton – there was some time for relaxation during the mammoth Anglo-American-French-Egyptian operation to clear the waterway to the East, closed since 1967, of the detritus of the Arab-Israeli wars of 1967 and 1973. But not much...

Since April thousands of explosives and other military hardware had been found and detonated by the Royal Navy, including 1,000lb, 750lb and 500lb bombs, mortars, anti tank and anti personnel mines, missile and aircraft wreckage, tanks and lorries loaded with ammunition.

Scorching heat, tedium and remoteness from the bright lights were the lot of the 260-strong RN team in the headquarters ship HMS Abdiel and the minehunters Maxton, Wilton and Bossington – and the Fleet Clearance Divers as they battled with "heat, flies, mosquitos and bad temper".

Among the more unpleasant discoveries of the hazardous operation had been bodies, including those of five Egyptian soldiers trapped in the wreckage of a truck. The task seemed endless – many of the bombs and missiles were bound to be buried too deep to be detected. "When the Pyramids are another 1,000 years older, there will still be bombs in the bottom of that bloody great ditch," one officer commented. [*October 1974*]

92

93

93 **A view from the Shell, like**

Two hundred feet up, in gale force winds and driving rain atop the Royal Dutch Shell Petroleum building, the company's photographer is joined by HMS Amazon's PR officer, Lieut. Malcolm Bird, to record the submarine Narwhal's arrival at Amsterdam on film. HMS Ajax was also included in a five-day visit to the Dutch capital. [*January 1975*]

94 **Tribal gathering**

HMS Tartar (foreground) and HMS Eskimo are captured exercising in the West Indies in a rare shot of two Tribal-Class frigates together.

They followed up with inspections on the Atlantic Fleet Weapons Range and at the US Naval Base at Roosevelt Roads, Puerto Rico. [*February 1975*]

95

94

95 *Jura goes offshore*

The Royal Navy's first offshore patrol ship to combine the roles of fishery and oil rig protection, HMS Jura, had commissioned at her home base, HMS. Lochinvar, Port Edgar. The Jura, was the Department of Fisheries (Scotland) fishery protection ship, built at Aberdeen in 1972. She was on loan to the Navy's Offshore Squadron and since March 3 had been at Rosyth having naval communications equipment and a 44mm Bofors gun installed.

Then commanded by Lieut.-Cdr T F N Donald, she is pictured leaving Port Edgar for trials before her first patrol.

The first RN ship to bear the name had been an Isles Class trawler built in 1941 and sunk in the western Mediterranean in January 1943. [*May 1975*]

96 *Just a bunch of squares*

HMS Glamorgan, wearing the flag of the Flag Officer Second Flotilla (Rear-Admiral John Fieldhouse) heads ships of the 8th Frigate Squadron. In their round-the-world group deployment, the ships went through the Suez Canal on their way to the Far East to carry out exercises with many foreign and Commonwealth navies. They would be away from the UK for nine months.

The ships' companies departed safe in the knowledge that the Royal Navy's 'square rig' – "pride of the mums, delight of the dollies and as traditional as 'Hearts of Oak'" – was to be retained as the sailors' dress uniform.

As far back as 1971 various fashion ideas had been displayed to a somewhat amused and occasionally sarcastic Senior Service, leading to the creation of three styles which were tried in the Fleet for 12 months. But evolution, not revolution, had been agreed as the most sensible solution. The Queen approved a modernised version which retained the essential features while incorporating a number of improvements. Henceforth trousers would be flared from the knee with vertical, rather than the old horizontal creases; velcro fastenings secured the collar to the jumper, which had integral black 'silk' facings; and separate black silk, lanyard and tapes were dispensed with. Issue of the new uniform would begin in 1977. [*September 1975*]

97 *Sheer escapism*

Officers and ratings of the Canadian submarine HMCS Ojibwa watch as the Vickers Oceanics submersible VOL L1

96

97

is lowered into the Gareloch for the Royal Navy's first trials of a commercial input to submarine rescue operations. HMS Otter was also involved in these tests, in which the submersible made a free approach to a submarine lying disabled on the sea bed, locked onto a transfer port, and allowed stranded personnel to make their escape 'dry'.

Deep Submergence Rescue Vehicle couplers were being fitted to all Royal Navy submarines – although the Service would continue to rely mainly on its well-proven system in which men are trained in the techniques of making free ascents in survival suits from a submarine's escape chamber. [*October 1975*]

98 **Tartar travels up top**

HMS Tartar off the south coast of Bear Island during a deep water fishery patrol – which extended as far north as Spitzbergen and off the Murmansk coast in the Barents Sea. Visits were made to Hammerfest Tromso and Bergen during the ship's time 'up top'. [*December 1975*]

98

99 **Gan, but not forgotten**

A final farewell – HMS Rothesay sails through the Gan channel, the last British warship to visit the familiar staging post in the Indian Ocean before the closure of the RAF station on the island.

On solo detachment from the Group Three deployment, the Rothesay took into care the large collection of wall plaques from Royal Navy and Royal Marines units which had used the anchorage facilities over the years, during which Gan had featured on the itinerary of countless servicemen and their families heading to and from the Far East. [*February 1976*]

99

100 **Magnificent seven**

All the modern types of helicopter currently operated by the Royal Navy were seen in this photograph, taken off Portland by LA Roger Forbes. From the top, they were: The Sea King, then the world's most advanced anti-submarine helicopter, also used for search and rescue operations; the Wessex Mk 3, an anti-submarine aircraft; the Wessex Mk 5 troop carrier; the Wessex Mk 1, used mainly for search and rescue; the Lynx, due to replace the Wasp in many ships; the Wasp, still operating from many of the Royal Navy's frigates; and the Gazelle, the Fleet Air Arm's new basic helicopter trainer.

Missing from the line-up was the Whirlwind – which entered service with the Royal Navy in the early Fifties and therefore could not be classified as 'modern', although it was still playing a vital role in SAR operations. [*March 1976*]

100

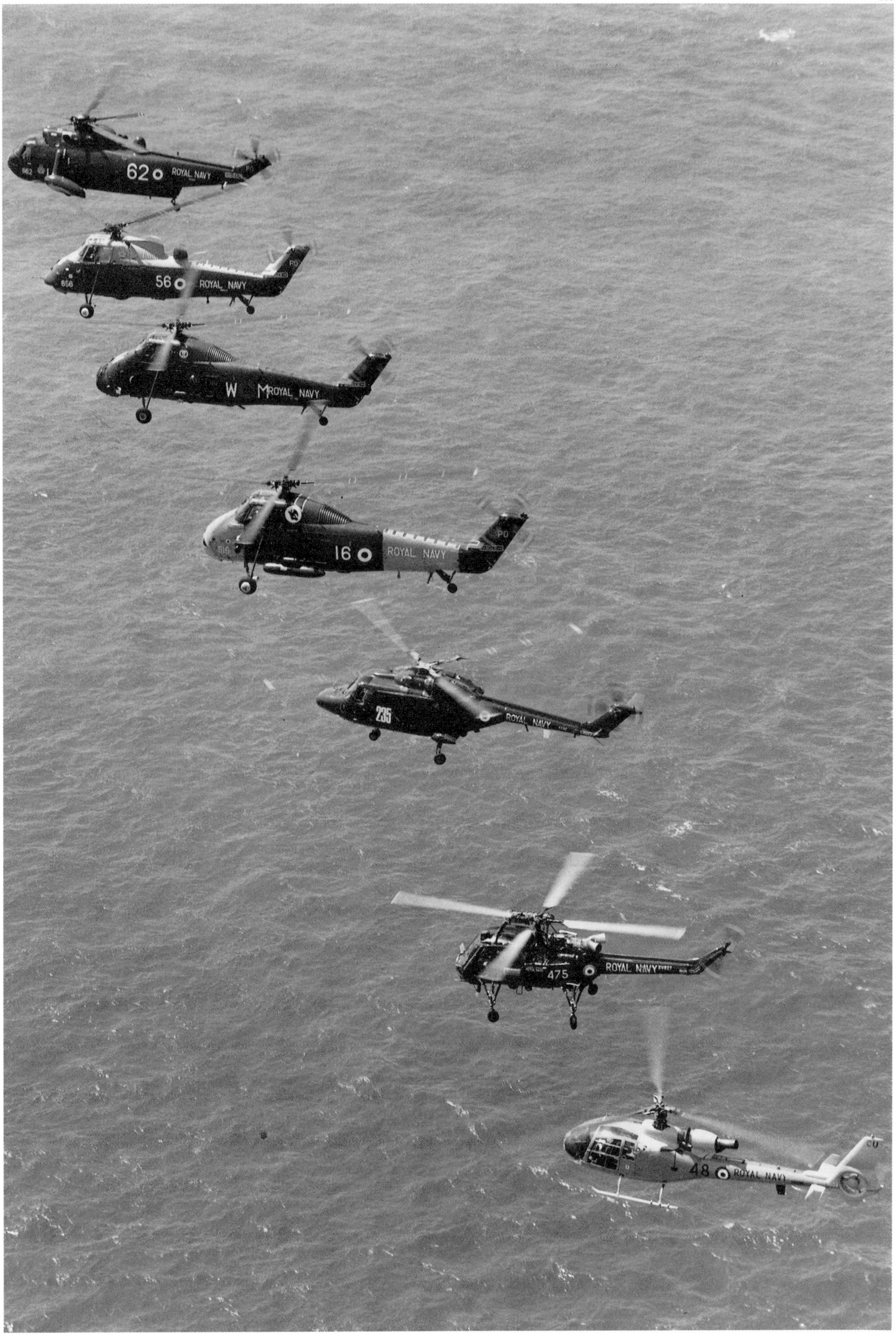

101

101 **Mind the paint, sir...**

Several amusing signals passed between HMY Britannia and HMS Bronington after Lieut. The Prince of Wales took command of the minehunter on February 9. From the Flag Officer Royal Yachts (Rear Admiral H P Janion) came the following message:

"The Royal Yachtsmen old and new
Humbly send these words to you:
May fair winds and good fortune be
Forever in your company.
But what about, oh captain new,
A Ton class painted royal blue?"

To which the Prince – whose humourous talents were already known to the public through his participation in undergraduate revue at Cambridge University and his friendship with arch-Goons Spike Milligan, Peter Sellers and Harry Secombe – responded in fine (actually rather better) literary style:

"To all those Yachties old and new
For such a message of good cheer
Which I shall always hold most dear
– My gratitude is more than due
Perhaps I should just mention here
That if we meet at sea this year
Be sure to keep your fenders out
Lest your paint gets spread
about." [*March 1976*]

102 ... **Bronington's bearded boss books in at Barry**

Prince Charles – displaying a short-lived experiment with a sailorly 'full set' – signs the civic visitors' book during the Bronington's four-day visit to Barry in company with HMS Bildeston. [*June 1976*]

102

103 **Wasp stripped for traction**

A Spanish climber whose leg was broken 900 ft up the sheer face of the Rock of Gibraltar, was rescued by HMS Bacchante's Wasp helicopter. The operation took three hours and at times the aircraft's rotor blades waved within inches of the rock face.

The Bacchante was asked to help after the climber had been stranded for 24 hours. The ascent on which the man lay is recognised as being one of the most difficult in the world and the progress of a team of rescue climbers was slow.

After studying the rock face through binoculars, Lieut. Chris Chadwick took off in the Wasp with Leading aircrewman Jeff Coward. They made several circuits, each time getting closer to the rock, until the helicopter was 25 ft from the rescue team.

It was necessary, however, to return to North Front Airfield on several occasions, to top up with fuel and lighten the aircraft by stripping out flotation gear, seats and doors.

The position of the injured man ruled out a 'hi-line' transfer and the rescuers eventually dragged him to a small ledge from which he could be taken off by standard winch transfer.

• Here the climber's ordeal is nearly over. With his broken leg strapped up, he is taken into the Wasp before being whisked away to hospital. Crowds watched the rescue from vantage points above and below the action – and the day's excitement was brought to a happy conclusion with a half-hour tribute to his saviours on Gibraltar Television. [*June 1976*]

103

104 **Smoky Mo signals her return**

HMS Mohawk's ceremonial entry into Portland Harbour produced this 'Tribal' smoke signal effect – prompting some witty comments about "two-stroke frigates". After sea trials and a visit to Guernsey, the Mohawk had arrived for work-up, pleased to be running again after a year in dockyard hands at Devonport. [*August 1976*]

104

105

105 **We are sailing...**

Straight from the American bicentennial bonanza – for which 650 sailors formed up on the flight deck to spell out the tribute "1776–1976" for her entry to Fort Lauderdale – HMS Ark Royal returned to the UK to bask in the success of her apotheosis as the subject of a ten-part BBC series "Sailor", a highly controversial warts-and-all documentary of life in the Senior Service that broke new ground in portraying the stresses and strains of a career in the Royal Navy.

Though scenes of sailors letting of steam during a last night ashore raised eyebrows among the Naval Establishment, the fact that they were set alongside episodes of solid professionalism – as in a dramatic rescue of an American sailor suffering from appendicitis who was washed off a submarine by a large wave while waiting to be lifted off by helicopter – only served to concentrate public interest in what was obviously not just another run-of-the-mill propaganda exercise. Thus criticism was easily deflected: "This was no 'wardroom show', but splendidly balanced entertainment full of sailor activity, humour, thrills, drama and human interest".

"If the opening installments set a few eyes popping, any doubts will fade in the succeeding weeks," Navy News stated confidently. And they did – "Sailor" became the yardstick against which all Service documentaries are measured to this day.

Rod Stewart's smash hit anthem "Sailing" set the scene so aptly that many viewers imagined it had been written especially for the occasion. [*August 1976*]

106 **Battle with the Atlantic**

Wessex and Scout aircraft of 845 Naval Squadron were lashed on the deck of HMS Fearless during a Force 8 gale while taking part in Exercise Team Work in northern waters – this picture taken during a heavy roll to starboard.

The amphibious ship was taking part in a massive NATO exercise covering almost the entire 12 million square miles of the Atlantic Command and involving 80,000 Alliance personnel and all three major NATO commands.

More than 200 ships, 30 submarines and 900 aircraft took part, the main object being to test plans designed to provide for the defence of Western Europe.

In the background is the Royal Fleet Auxiliary tanker Tidespring. [*October 1976*]

106

107 **Bond ship stirred but not shaken**

The presence of a film crew shooting sequences for the new James Bond film 'The Spy Who Loved Me' was providing a fair measure of excitement for HMS Fearless when a real-life drama took over....

Half-way through the first shot on a perfect Sunday morning off Malta, the assault ship turned away to go to the aid of the 6,500 ton Greek cargo ship Mostros Vassos Atene, in which an engine room fire had spread rapidly through accommodation spaces and superstructure.

Firefighting and damage control parties were put on board and as the fires gained in intensity one of the first tasks was to get rid of a large quantity of inflammable deck cargo – including 80 five-gallon drums of oxidising acid, three drums of benzene, two tons of paint and no fewer than 23 tons of gas lighter fluid.

Later the Greek ship developed a 'loll' owing to the amount of water being pumped into her, but by now the Fearless had her secured alongside and was able to hold her.

In late afternoon the fires appeared to be out, and next morning the Royal Navy ship was able to hand over to harbour tugs. However, some fire and damage control parties remained on board most of the day while the film unit calmly completed their task.

Before leaving they sent the following message. "From James Bond film unit to HMS Fearless. Many thanks for a good shoot. A highly eventful week when many were stirred but none were shaken. Signed 007." [*December 1976*]

107

108 **Orpheus, king of the underwater look**

HMS Keppel, photographed through the periscope of HMS Orpheus with the same line overlap technique used for coastline surveillance.

Cameras have been used in Royál Navy submarines since the earliest days –the first operational picture was a view of Constantinople during the Gallipoli campaign – and the processing methods involved would be familiar to any amateur photographer. A standard SLR camera body is clamped to the periscope's eyepiece and uses the instrument's own lenses to obtain the picture – but the entire crew's dedication and teamwork are employed to maintain depth and speed in order to approach the subject with the utmost stealth, ensuring that the periscope is exposed above the surface for the minimum time to avoid detection. Even more delicate are 'underwater look' operations to photograph the underside of a warship or another submarine. Single shots or panoramic views made up from a series of exposures can be taken – or 'stereo pairs' using two photographs taken from slightly different vantage points which can later be viewed to produce a three dimensional effect which gives detailed intelligence information. The picture was taken by Lieut. Christopher Waters (seen here in the submarine's control room) who won the 1976 Periphot competition. [*February 1977*]

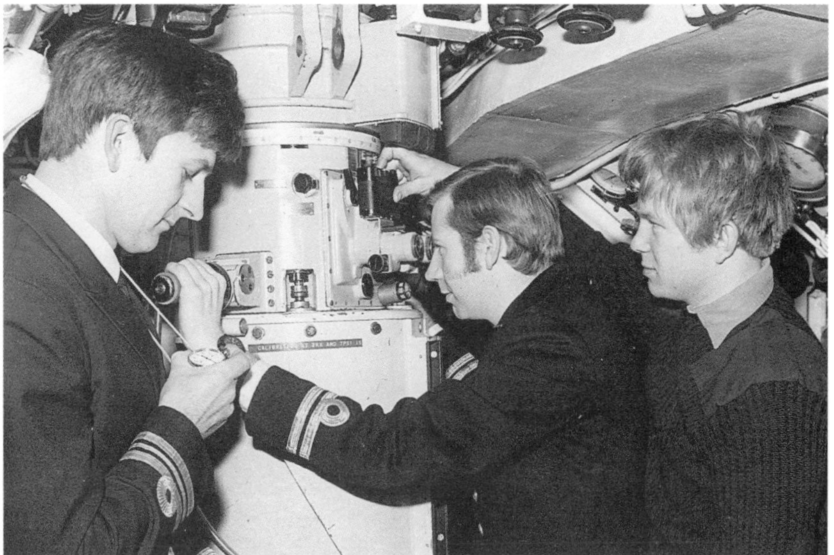

108a

108b

109 *Vernon's gift of the Nile*

Stone by stone, the Navy recovers the Gate of Diocletian – at the end of this month RN and Egyptian divers were completing the task of salvaging an ancient Roman monument from the waters of the Nile near Philae.

Built in the 3rd century AD, the two remaining archways were submerged with the completion of the Aswan Dam in 1970. Now it was planned to re-erect the huge gate on the island of Agilkia – with the help of divers from HMS Vernon.

They had to move tons of mud, chip away concrete placed on the monument half a century earlier, measure and mark every stone and secure them for removal by flotation bags.

• *Below, right:* Led by Lieut.-Cdr Ed Thompson, members of the RN diving team stroll in the courtyard of the Temple of Kom Ombo, 26 miles from Aswan.

109c

109a 109b

• *Above:* Thumbs up from a diver – beneath the flotation bag is a stone from the Gate of Diocletian, to be rebuilt on the island of Agilkia (background) which had been reshaped to resemble the original island of Philae. [*April 1977*]

110

110 *Sea Devon's 6,000 hours*

The Sea Devon XK 895 – which had lately celebrated its 21st birthday – flies over St Michael's Mount, Cornwall. Based at RN air station Culdrose, the aircraft had seen service at Yeovilton, Malta, Lee-on-Solent and Lossiemouth, where it began life in 1956, and had since logged 6,200 flying hours. Although primarily a communications aircraft, the Sea Devon had been used on various exercises and had recently returned to Hampshire to assist with fishery protection patrols. [*May 1977*]

111 *Browned off bears*

An ice-removal party at work on HMS Birmingham off Bear Island during trials to prove that Type 42 destroyers

could operate successfully in Arctic conditions.

Before embarking from Portsmouth, bridge screen and other forward surfaces had been liberally coated with greasy brown anti-frost material and every moveable item of equipment on the upper deck was shrouded in vinyl sheeting or smeared with grease.

Soon after joining HMS Arrow in the trials area a pipe was made to announce that a polar bear had been spotted taking angry swipes at the Type 21 frigate's helicopter as it disturbed the Arctic peace. *[May 1977]*

112 **Silver Jubilee Review at Spithead**

The Queen passes HMS Ark Royal in HMY Britannia at the start of her Silver Jubilee Review of Royal Navy and Commonwealth ships assembled at Spithead.

The Royal Yacht is followed by HMS Birmingham and the helicopter support ship RFA Engadine, loaded with Press observers

There were 175 ships in the lines with 30,000 men embarked for the biggest Spithead spectacular since the Coronation Review in 1953. Ark Royal was the largest RN warship to be seen during the Review column's 15 mile circuit, which included representatives from 17 other nations. One of the most distinctive was the frigate HMNLS Tromp (foreground, left) nicknamed 'Kojak' because of the huge radome above her bridge. *[July 1977]*

111

112

113

113 Guano problem in "Guzz Garage"

If it made sense to service the family car under cover, there had to be a case for looking after warships in the comfort of the 'Guzz Garage' the monumental frigate complex newly opened at Devonport.

An impression of its mammoth proportions is gained from this picture featuring the Leander Class HMS Galatea, which became the first frigate to start a six-month indoor refit there. She moved into No 6 dock as part of the official opening ceremony, having earlier made a successful trial run into No 7.

A trio of warships could now be serviced simultaneously in the warm and dry of the towering covered docks supported by six 175 ft reinforced concrete towers – Nelson's Column could stand inside each of them.

Only one drawback – it had been observed that the ships' decks were subject to aerial attack from birds who were likewise attracted to the comfort of the complex. [*October 1977*]

115

114 **Beefing up the mine busters**

HMS Gavinton leads HMS Brinton and HMS Kedleston past the hovercraft BH7 during Exercise Roast Beef – an operation to clear practice mines around the eastern and southern coasts of England. On the way, five live second world war mines were also unearthed and destroyed – leaving fishermen pursuing their livelihood off Essex a little easier in their minds.

Modern mines were more complex and harder to destroy. Sophisticated detection methods had been developed since these mahogany-hulled Tonclass vessels were built in the late 1950s and the first of the new glass-reinforced plastic mine countermeasures vessels, the 625-ton HMS Brecon, was due to enter service in a year's time. [*November 1977*]

114

116a

115 **Antelope enters the Ark**

HMS Antelope alongside HMS Ark Royal for a jackstay transfer in the Caribbean. The Type 21 frigate had been acting as plane guard for night flying off the carrier, having done duty as Belize guardship. [*June 1978*]

116 **Fire over Brum and Belfast**

The Firemen's strike had kept 4,000 Royal Navy and Royal Marines personnel on duty over the festive season, manning "Green Goddess" service fire engines throughout the UK and tackling emergency calls to hotels, warehouses, garages, flats, oil depots and simple chimney fires.

Belfast posed special problems. Each time the call went out, the whole area involved had to be checked for bombs before the fire fighting team could go into action. Here the joint service group included a detachment from HMS Sultan, four groups working in the chief city of Northern Ireland with another in Londonderry.

• *Right:* Delta Two, manned by sailors from HMS Dolphin, heads out into the night to tackle a blaze in Birmingham. [*January 1978*]

116b

117 Sea Harrier debuts –

Making its international debut at Farnborough was the first Sea Harrier for the Royal Navy, piloted by British Aerospace chief test pilot John Farley who demonstrated launches from a 15 degree ski jump ramp erected by the Royal Engineers.

HMS Invincible, first of the new "command cruisers", would have a seven degree ramp, later to be enhanced, and it was planned to fit HMS Hermes during her refit scheduled in the following year. The first Sea Harrier squadron, 800, was to form in 1980. [*October 1978*]

118 – as a Sea King ditches

Meanwhile a Sea King helicopter of 814 Squadron arrived on board the Hermes in no less spectacular fashion. Forced to ditch in the sea off Lundy when a major gear box oil leak occurred during a mail run from Plymouth, the aircraft – thanks to a calm sea, the skill of pilot Lieut. Keith Dudley, and inbuilt flotation bags – was safely restored to the flight deck. [*October 1978*]

117

118a

118b

118c

118d

120

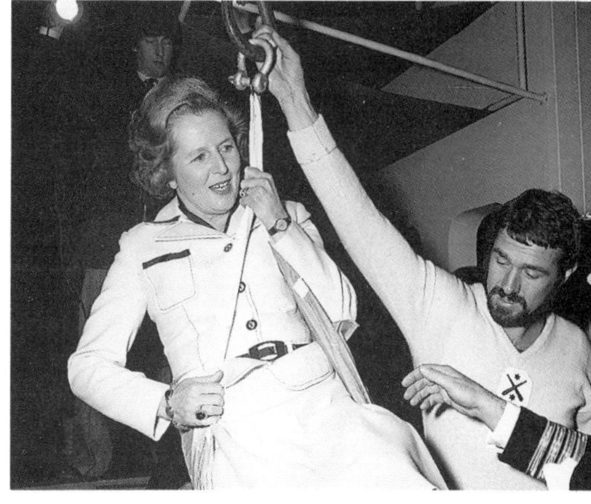

119

119 RN't I brave?'

Mrs Thatcher samples a jackstay transfer across the pool at the 25th London International Boat Show, assisted by LPT Bob Aindow and RN Director of Public Relations Captain Derek Blacker. She was one of 5,000 visitors who made the crossing – and received certificates and stickers printed with the legend "I've been jackstayed! RN't I brave?" *[February 1979]*

120 All-metric, all-missile

A landmark in modern warship designs came with the acceptance into service at Devonport of HMS Broadsword, first of the Type 22 frigates – also the first ship to be built around an all-missile main armament system and the first all-metric warship.

Her weapons fit comprised the Seawolf anti-missile and anti-aircraft point defence missile system: four Exocet surface-to-surface missile launchers; two 40mm Bofors guns for close range action; two sets of triple torpedo tubes; and a Lynx multi-purpose helicopter. *[March 1979]*

121

121 Doing the Tank

More than 20,000 escapes in 25 years – that was the proud record of the Submarine Escape Training Tank at HMS Dolphin, prominent in this aerial view of the Submarine Service's alma mater at Gosport, Hants.

The Tank Still led the world in escape techniques – and many of the world's navies continued to send their men to practise in the 100ft water-filled tower, making two ascents of nine metres and one of 18 metres with standard escape apparatus – breathing equipment and a buoyant, insulated suit – before they made the ultimate 30 metre shoot to the surface at 10ft per second.

It is still said that most novices are terrified when they first "do the Tank" – and then want to do it again... *[July 1979]*

122

122 **Life after 40**

One of the most famous Naval vessels still afloat – MTB 102 – was a star attraction when she appeared for Portsmouth Navy Days. The 42-year-old boat, Vosper prototype for hundreds of World War II craft, was visited by more than 5,000 sightseers, including former wartime crew members. The renovated craft was owned by Blofield and Blundall Sea Scouts unit, near Norwich. [*October 1979*]

123 **Fife lightens Dominica's darkest hour**

HMS Fife comes into Portsmouth streaming her paying off pennant – ten days overdue after her epic, island-saving mission in the wake of Hurricane David. Her ship's company had performed a near-miracle in getting the devastated Caribbean island of Dominica back on its feet after the worst hurricane recorded this century, with winds up to 150 knots, had left scenes of nuclear style ruin there. Not a tree had been left standing, half the buildings had been demolished and only a small number of those left still had roofs.

The people were immobilised by shock; savage injuries had been caused by corrugated iron scything from the buildings; the hospital was shattered, there was no fresh water, no power, no communications.

But within four days the Fife had restored the hospital, cleared tons of rubble which had blocked the reservoir, and re-opened a road to the airport. The ship's company themselves went on food and water rationing working up to 18 hours a day under the threat of a second storm – Hurricane Frederick.

A message from Dominica's acting president, Mr Jenner Armour, was passed to the ship by The Queen: "They arrived on our ravaged shores at our darkest hour and lit the first beacon of hope. Their relief efforts were ceaseless and untiring, their devotion to duty a shining example of true friendship in our hour of need." [*October 1979*]

123

124a

124 **Murder most foul**

Ratings from HMS Mercury carry the coffin of Admiral of the Fleet Earl Mountbatten of Burma – murdered, together with his grandson Nicholas and the Dowager Lady Brabourne, by IRA terrorists in Northern Ireland.

He was buried at Romsey, near his home at Broadlands, after a funeral service in Westminster Abbey, where the field gun carriage bearing his coffin through the streets of London was the one, kept at HMS Excellent, used at the funerals of Queen Victoria, King Edward VII, King George V, King George VI. It was in every sense a Naval funeral – as befitted one who regarded his years in the Service as "the core of his professional life". At the end of May he had paid what was to be his last visit to a Royal Navy warship – the nuclear- powered Fleet submarine HMS Superb. In the early 1920s he had briefly served the submarine K3 – and the Submarine Service dolphins badge always sat proudly above the deep rows of his decorations. [*October 1979*]

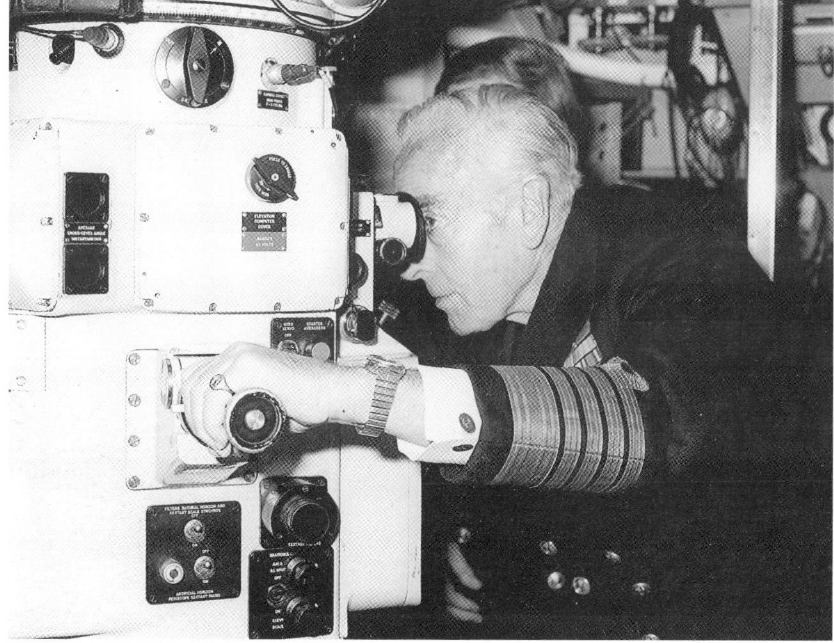

124b

The 1980s

JUNE 1982 10p

GUNS AT DAWN

Gunsmoke drifts away from a Royal Navy Rothesay-class frigate as a line of warships bombard Argentine positions at Grytviken on South Georgia. This dramatic picture was taken from a County-class guided missile destroyer on the morning of April 25 as Royal Marines and Army troops were landed by helicopter to recapture the island 23 days after it had fallen into Argentine hands.

Only casualty during the two-hour operation was an Argentine sailor who was wounded in the leg and later had the leg amputated. The article of surrender was signed on board HMS Plymouth the following day.

● More pictures in Pages 9, 10 and 40.

Invasion

AIR ATTACK ON SHIPS

AS Navy News went to press on May 22, first details were emerging of a major landing by British forces in the Falkland Islands.

At the same time, it was announced from London that five Task Force ships had been damaged, two seriously, in heavy air attacks. There were casualties on both sides.

Royal Marines Commandos and paratroopers established a firm bridgehead after several landings and raids in different parts of the islands.

A statement said the British troops were ashore in substantial numbers with artillery, air defence weapons and other heavy equipment disembarked from the Task Force ships.

AIRCRAFT DESTROYED

British Harriers and missiles had destroyed 16 Argentine aircraft, plus two helicopters on the ground. But it was learned that one Harrier was missing and two British helicopters were lost.

Reporters with a ship which launched one of the landings described a four-hour operation including naval bombardments of enemy shore positions, followed by wave upon wave of attacks by Argentine fighters and bombers.

During the preparations for the British landings, a Royal Navy Sea King ditched with 30 men on board. Nine were rescued, one body was recovered, and 20 were missing, presumed dead.

Ambulance brigade

Dressed up in their new "sea ambulance" livery, HMS Hydra (background) and HMS Herald carry out a jackstay transfer on their way to the South Atlantic. The picture was taken by LA(Phot) T. Butcher from the Herald. See special feature in centre pages.

125 **Sad duty for Scimitar**

Sea patrols operated by L Company of 42 Commando RM proved highly successful during 42's two month spell in Hong Kong. In all, they caught 1,564 illegal immigrants from China at sea, many of them intercepted in Rigid Raider craft. After they were taken off their sampans were usually destroyed by holing, ramming or explosion to avoid hazard to navigation. Here, the end of one is supervised by the fast patrol boat HMS Scimitar.

It was a task no-one enjoyed. "I.I.s" were sometimes brought aboard with terrible shark injuries; there were instances of mothers, knowing they were to be repatriated, thrusting children into sailors' arms in the hope that they at least might be allowed to stay; often individuals were recognised as having been round the course before five or six times. In one month 14,000 were passed back. Hong Kong remains a glittering, teeming target for thousands of refugees from neighbouring countries which it cannot hope to sustain. [*January 1980*]

125

126 **Two eras, nose to tail**

A moment of aerial nostalgia as a Fairey Swordfish of World War II vintage shares the limelight with a Sea Harrier during a fly-past at the RN air station Yeovilton. The two aircraft represented 46 years of Rolls Royce Bristol Pegasus aero engine development, which had advanced flying speeds from 120 mph to 600 knots plus. [*March 1980*]

126

127

127 **Disaster in the North Sea**

The saddest 36 hours in the log of HMS Lindisfarne came with the Aleksander L Kielland disaster in the North Sea, in which more than 100 men died.

The fishery protection vessel was the first warship on the scene after the capsize of the Norwegian accommodation rig. To get there she had steamed 180 miles at top speed across the Ekofisk oilfield – and then her main contribution to the gruelling search by a little fleet of oil rig craft and fishing vessels, directed by RAF Nimrod with the help of the Dutch frigate HNLMS Overjssel, was the transfer of bodies to the main oil rig, using her 85 hp sea boat.

819 Naval Air Squadron, based at Prestwick, was also involved in the operation. [*May 1980*]

128 **Speedy takes wing**

HMS Speedy, the Navy's experimental hydrofoil, was commissioned at HMS Vernon. The Rt Hon Vere Cochrane, great-great grandson of Lord Cochrane who commanded the first HMS Speedy in 1801, presented a picture of that ship in battle.

Built by Boeing Marine Systems of Seattle, the new Speedy lived up to her name, her 43 knots making her the fastest ship in the Fleet as she "flew" through the water under the power of her two gas turbines, her retractable hydroplanes acting like wings to lift the hull clear of the surface. [*July 1980*]

128

129 **Lucia honours Glasgow**

HMS Glasgow alongside at St Lucia – the twisted, devastated building telling the story of Huricane Allen. Diverted to the West Indian island on her way home from a spell of duty as Belize guardship, the destroyer found winds of up to 170 mph had killed and injured many inhabitants, destroyed vital services and severely damaged homes and crops. Over a five day period, Glasgow sailors, helped by the ship's Lynx helicopters, treated more than 300 casualties and evacuated the severe cases to hospital. Power, water and hospital services were restored and crop damage surveyed in dawn to dusk missions. When the Glasgow finally sailed, Prime Minister Allan Lovisy requested that the ship be permitted to fly the St Lucia flag on special occasions as a mark of honour for her work.

129a

Bananas were not left out of Glasgow's salvage operation – about 90 per cent of St Lucia's crop was ruined in the catastrophe. [*September 1980*]

129b

130

130 **Thar she blows**

Smoke screen tactics were NOT being reintroduced into the Fleet. This spectacular picture showed HMS Ariadne blowing soot on flashing up for the first time after her Gibraltar refit. [*October 1980*]

Mr John Nott – who would propose drastic cuts for the Royal Navy on the eve of the Falklands War – became Secretary of State for Defence in January 1981.

131

132a

131 Refits quicker by rail

HMS Gavinton becomes the first ship to be synchrolifted out of the water and shunted into Rosyth's new refitting complex. The £12m refit shop would revolutionise working conditions in the dockyard, where small ship refits had previously taken place in the open and in floating docks in the main basin.

Rosyth could now programme refits more precisely – free from interruptions by wind and rain. The synchrolift could pluck mine countermeasures vessels and small patrol ships from the water, trundle them along a 400 ft railway line, squirt marine growth off their hulls with high pressure water jets, and park them snugly into a massive five berth "garage". [*December 1980*]

132 First RN submarine found

Holland I, the Royal Navy's first submarine which sank on her way to the breaker's yard in 1913, was found off Eddystone Lighthouse.

The minesweeper HMS Bossington first made sonar contact with the wreck, later confirmed by the diving trials ship Seaforth Clansman as the first of the Holland Class built in 1901–02.

The boat – with many of her interior fittings miraculously intact, including a splendid porcelain "Doulton's No 612" WC, complete with wooden seat – was later raised and put on permanent display at the Submarine Museum at Gosport.

Holland I remains the only surviving example of the American design built under license by Vickers at Barrow-in-Furness, still the lead builders of RN submarines in the nuclear age.

A nine-man petrol-engine and battery driven craft, only 63 ft long with a displacement of 120 tons, she could manage a top speed of nine knots surfaced and six knots submerged and could dive to only 100 ft. Her single torpedo tube, ordered by the Admiralty to be "mangled" when she was sold for scrap, was also mysteriously intact, its heavy brass rear door shut tight. It had never been called upon to fire a shot in anger – to the relief of one of her last COs, 90-year-old Captain Ronald Blacklock, who recalled that she had been "impossible to control in in any kind of sea".

But her distinctive cigar-shaped hull proved to be the ideal submarine configuration, not fully appreciated by submarine designers until the arrival of the modern "nukes". [*May 1981*]

134

133 Tussle with a trawler

HMS Alderney was involved in one of the most dramatic fishery incidents since the Cod War when she tried to escort an offending French trawler into Grimsby.

During a tense and hazardous day-long encounter the Jean Mermoz was alleged to have turned and headed for Boulogne after knives and an acetylene torch were used to threaten a boarding party. She later tried to ram the Alderney – as well as a Sea King helicopter from RAF Cottesmore called in to join the chase – and eventually collided with the Alderney after cutting across her bows.

Her master eventually accepted a tow – and the Frenchmen were heavily fined by Grimsby Magistrates Court, plus damages to the Alderney. [*August 1981*]

134 Manure to Muscat

HMS Euryalus kicked up a major stink while on patrol in the Gulf of Oman – by rescuing a cargo of cow dung.

MV Dhahi, carrying 240 tons of "natural fertiliser" from Karachi to Kuwait, had drifted helplessly with engine failure for 24 hours when the frigate intercepted her radio calls. It took her only an hour to pick up the unmistakable scent of her quarry. A line was passed and the Euryalus towed the dung ship 70 miles to Muscat. When the boarding party returned their "close and prolonged contact with the nether products of a goodly portion of Pakistan's bovine inhabitants was immediately obvious" – and they had to be hosed down before Euryalus could breathe again. [*December 1981*]

132b

133

135 **Viking funeral for Rapid**

One of the last of Britain's wartime escorts was torpedoed in the Western Approaches – almost 40 years after she began her career. HMS Rapid fell victim to the submarine HMS Onyx after being battered as a target ship for the latest generation of missiles carried by RN surface vessels.

A Viking funeral might seem a more dignified end for a warship than slow dismemberment in the scrapyard – the emergency class destroyer could be seen as donating her body for science. But it is hard to view these occasions and photographs like this one have often invited protest from members of former ship's companies.

HMS Rapid saw war service in the South Atlantic and the Far East and action off Sumatra and in the offensive on Burma in 1945. During bombardment of the Andaman Islands she was severely damaged and had to be towed to safety.

She was converted after the war as a first-rate anti-submarine frigate (Type 15) and again, in 1967 after a spell in reserve, to fulfil the role as HMS Caledonia's training ship. She went out of service in the early Seventies. [*February 1982*]

135a 135b

The Falklands War

136 **Guns at dawn**

Smoke drifts away from HMS Plymouth as a line of warships bombard Argentine positions at Grytviken on South Georgia while Royal Marines join Army troops landed by helicopter to recapture the island 23 days after it had fallen into Argentine hands.

The article of surrender was signed on board the Rothesay Class frigate the following day. A decade later she has been saved by the Warship Preservation Trust as a permanent memorial to the Royal Navy's most celebrated post World War II operation. [*June 1982*]

137 **The end of the Antelope**

HMS Antelope explodes in San Carlos Bay, East Falklands. Press Association photographer Martin Cleaver's dramatic picture was one of the most potent images of the sea-borne trauma of Operation Corporate

The Type 21 frigate claimed shooting down two Argentine aircraft in the attack on her before she was struck by two 1,000lb bombs.

An attempt to defuse one of these was unsuccessful and the explosion tore a huge hole in the ship's side, starting major fires in the both engine rooms and several other compartments. These got dangerously close to several magazines – and ten minutes after the last man followed the order to abandon ship the Antelope was torn apart by a huge explosion. Next morning all that remained of her was the bow and stern pointing upwards. [*July 1982*]

136
137

138

139

140

138 **Hitting the beaches**

Landing craft moving towards the beaches from the fog-shrouded assault ship HMS Fearless, which with her sister ship HMS Intrepid played a vital part in the campaign for the islands. [*July 1982*]

139 **Cardiff adopts 'Tiger Bay'**

Among the spoils of war in the Falklands was the German-built patrol craft Islas Malvinas – captured in Port Stanley and promptly renamed HMS Tiger Bay. She became the first command for Lieut. Simon Hambrook from the Type 42 destroyer HMS Cardiff, and so took her name from the famous dockside area of the Welsh capital. He found her "in a dreadful mess" but in sound condition and hardly damaged. A similar craft, partially destroyed in Harrier attacks, was used to provide spare parts. [*August 1982*]

140 **Conqueror flies the Jolly Roger**

Most controversial of all actions in the Falklands War was the sinking of the Argentine cruiser General Belgrano. Whether or not the Belgrano and her escorting destroyers had posed an immediate threat to the Task Force would be debated for years afterwards – but the commanding officer of the nuclear-powered Fleet submarine, HMS Conqueror Cdr. Christopher Wreford-Brown, was in no doubt as he arrived home at the Clyde Submarine Base.

He had attacked on direct orders from Fleet headquarters, he said, and though he regretted the loss of life, he had "saved a considerable loss of life from the British Task Force and a potential threat from Exocet missiles with which she was armed."

He is seen here on the extreme right of the submarine's fin as she came

141

alongside at Faslane. There was some criticism, too, over the display of a Jolly Roger – the skull-and-crossbones flag traditionally flown by RN submarines to denote their successes on war patrols and adopted in defiance of the Admiralty's own early branding of submarines as "pirates". Depicted on the Conqueror's flag were a skull and crossed torpedoes, the silhouette of a warship, a dagger denoting a clandestine operation and an atomic symbol to underline the submarine's nuclear propulsion plant. She had been at sea for 90 days, much of the time submerged around the Falkland Islands. It was largely thanks to the threat her presence there imposed that the Argentine Navy's chief units kept their distance throughout most of the campaign. [*August 1982*]

141 **Cardiff home from the war**

HMS Cardiff sails into Portsmouth to an ecstatic welcome from families and friends on her return from the Falklands. She had joined the Battle Group on May 26 after a fast passage south in company with HMS Bristol.She was involved in the air defence of the group, shelled Argentine troop positions and was a guardship in the San Carlos Water area. She fired nine Sea Dart missiles and destroyed two aircraft.

When the Argentine garrison surrendered at Port Howard, West Falklands, the Cardiff was despatched to provide a visible presence. Her commanding officer, Captain Michael Harris, accepted the surrender there on June 15 with Lieut. Col M P J Hunt, Royal Marines. [*September 1982*]

142

142 **Apollo cracks up**

A wall of granite wave bears down on HMS Apollo. This picture, taken from the frigate's bridge, was a graphic illustration of the typical conditions being encountered by ships in the South Atlantic. It was the constant pounding by waves such as this that caused cracks in the Apollo's structure. Waves up to 60 ft high caused splits which spilled water into the Naafi – "completely reflavouring the Mars bars" – and the sonar control room, leading to light-hearted rumours that an indoor swimming pool was to open there... [*October 1982*]

143 **Falmouth in the Falklands**

Bleak winter greeted HMS Falmouth as she began her Falkland Islands patrol in mid-May. She is pictured passing Horse Rock, West Falkland 24 hours after conducting a memorial ceremony for HMS Ardent in San Carlos Water, when a wreath presented by the newly-formed Bollington Sea Cadet unit TS Ardent was placed over the spot where the sunken ship lies. [*July 1983*]

144 **£30,000 for point principle**

"The best of enemies" was how HMS Dumbarton Castle and the Danish trawler Sand Kirk were described in one of the most unusual confrontations to take place in the North Sea.

The Royal Navy fishery protection vessel found herself the focus of Europe when she was despatched to stem the invasion of British waters by the trawler owned and under the command of Euro-MP Kent Kirk.

He approached UK shores with the intention of testing a new law forbidding Danish vessels to fish within Britain's 12 mile limit and the Dumbarton Castle was there to meet him as he cast his nets off the North East coast. The small fishing vessel welcomed the boarding party with handshakes, however – and the best meal at the captain's table that her galley could provide.

Capt Kirk – acting, he said, on a point of principle – was escorted with his trawler into North Shields, where the next day he was fined £30,000 with £400 costs. [*February 1983*]

144

143

145 **Sirius first with towed array**

HMS Sirius, first of the Exocet-equipped Leander Class frigates to be fitted with towed array sonar submarine tracking gear, is seen here with her Lynx helicopter.

The winch had been located on a specially extended platform at the stern, while the absence of a large after radar aerial and the forward Seacat missile launcher and director made her even more distinctive among the Exocet-armed Leanders.

The Sirius's refit, started in May 1981, had been interrupted the following September when she was sent to patrol the South Atlantic. [*October 1983*]

146

146 **Bristol rover**

HMS Bristol sets course for home, half a world away to the north, after five months in the South Atlantic. Warships patrolling the protection zone around the Falklands were still being kept at a high state of readiness, eighteen months after the end of the fighting – for Argentina had never formally proclaimed a cessation of hostilities.

During her spell of duty at the head of the Task Unit, the Type 12 destroyer test fired all her weapons – including the first Ikara missile to be launched in the area.

After a brief stay at Madeira on the way back, the Bristol arrived at Portsmouth having logged 35,000 miles. [*January 1984*]

145

147

147 **RAAF are fair dinkum cobbers**

Typical of the Aussies' overwhelming welcome for Orient Express flagship HMS Invincible – seen here arriving at Sydney – was the Hercules air transport laid on by the Royal Australian Air Force to fly 90 of the carrier's sailors across the continent, so as not to mar a planned reunion with wives and girl friends.

The RAAF provided the special 2,000 mile flight after it was learned that the Invincible would have to leave for Singapore earlier than planned. As part of a long-standing arrangement, 90 women had flown from Britain to spend Christmas in Sydney. With the ship's premature departure it looked as if the reunion would have to be cut short but thanks to the airlift their holiday continued after the ship sailed.

Their menfo]k were left behind and later the RAAF flew them on to Perth, from where Sea King helicopters from the ship transferred them back on board as the carrier steamed past the Western Australia city. [*February 1984*]

148

148 **Aurora Orientalis**

Monsoon winds battered HMS Aurora for five weeks as she headed into the North Pacific for visits to Okinawa and South Korea.

The Aurora, one of the remaining ships of the Orient Express deployment, was accompanied by the Fleet tanker RFA Olmeda and the replenishment ship RFA Regent as she forged north to embark the Flag Officer First Flotilla, Rear Admiral Jeremy Black, at Okinawa.

Winds were steady at Force 6-7, gusting to Force 9 from the Philippines to Pusan, where temperatures dropped to minus 15 degrees C at night during the four day visit. Here the Aurora is shown roughing it during a RAS with RFA OLmeda en route. [*April 1984*]

149 **Sir Rex surveys his domain**

Dwarfed by her surroundings, HMS Endurance approaches the famous Lemaire Channel – the Antarctic Peninsula mainland to the right, Anvers Island to the left – as she steams north after taking part in "Winter Olympics" staged at Rothera, the British Antarctic Survey Base.

Sir Rex Hunt, High Commissioner of the British Antarctic Territories, was on board with Lady Hunt for a three week tour of his domain. Later the ice patrol ship rendezvoused with her Brazilian counterpart Barao de Teffe in sight of Elephant Island. The place and time were not without historical significance – almost exactly 68 years before Sir Ernest Shackleton landed there after his attempt to reach the South Pole had been thwarted when his ship Endurance was trapped in the Weddell Sea ice and crushed. [*April 1984*]

149

150 ***Red dusters dogged by the Reds***

HMS Euryalus leads ships of the Standing Naval Force Atlantic in the Cromarty Firth. The group was acting as escort to one of the largest gatherings of merchant shipping seen since the Second World War, Exercise Teamwork 84.

First task of the NATO squadron was to provide an anti-submarine barrier in the Iceland-Faroes Gap. Not only did they have to put up with a lot of "enemy" activity, but they were also subjected to considerable Soviet scrutiny – from the air, from surface ships and from submarines. Then they escorted a 29-ship convoy to Norway. Air and submarine "attacks" were made on the group and fast patrol boats had a go as the ships approached the Norwegian coast. Heavy weather slowed the convoy, so that its destination was changed from Trondheim to Alesund – where all six STANAVFORLANT ships managed a night alongside before escorting their charges back to Invergordon. [*May 1984*]

150

151

151 ***Carry on, Carron***

HMS Carron, second of the River class minesweepers, shows a useful turn of speed during trials. The Rivers were the first class of ship to be designed exclusively for Royal Naval Reserve use. Displacing 900 tons and armed with a 40mm Bofors anti-aircraft gun, they had a ship's company of 30. The Carron would replace HMS Venturer as the Severn Division training ship. [*August 1984*]

152 *Kitchen sink drama*

Warming to the task – with her foredeck awning giving some welcome relief – HMS Gavinton is pictured in the heat of the Gulf of Suez sun as she searches for mines after a series of explosions damaged over a score of merchant ships along the Red Sea.

When she detonated a Second World War German ground mine the explosion was seen from Adabiya, eight miles away.

Among the objects found littering the seabed were a 500lb bomb, a torpedo, 97 oil drums, a pair of aircraft wings – and a kitchen sink . . [*October 1984*]

153 *Foils for Liverpool*

Giving the impression of a large-scale power boat race, HMS Liverpool and the hydrofoil USS Aries cut through the waves somewhere between Belize and Nassau. The Type 42 destroyer was on passage when she spent some time operating with the Aries and her sister-craft USS Gemini. Armed with Harpoon surface-to-surface missiles, the Pegasus class hydrofoils had a top speed of 48 knots – when foil-borne their movement was so violent that the bridge crew had to be strapped into their seats. [*February 1985*]

152

153

154

154 *Uganda shows the scars*

Showing the ravages of life in the South Atlantic, the SS Uganda flies a paying off pennant as she leaves the Falklands carrying troops to Ascension Island.

After a career as a liner and a schools cruise ship, the Uganda had been chartered by the Ministry of Defence two years before as a troop ship – and had since shuttled more than 15,000 soldiers between the Falklands and Ascension – extensively used as a staging post during and after the 1982 conflict. Now she was on her way to be handed back to P & O at Falmouth. [*June 1985*]

155 *Nearly the last post for Upton*

One of the longest-serving of the Royal Navy's Ton class vessels was back at work – after a dockyard "nose job".

HMS Upton, launched almost 30 years before, had resumed her fishery protection duties after an extended refit which provided her with a new stem post. During her routine overhaul it was discovered that the wooden-hulled minesweeper was suffering from wet rot, so the docking was lengthened to allow the fitting of one of only two available spares.

Her return to duty in the Irish Sea this autumn was highlighted by an unusual firing of her 40/60mm Bofors gun. Because other warships were heavily committed to Exercise Ocean Safari, the Upton was the only RN vessel available in the Isle of Man area to provide a 15-gun salute for the entry of the new Governor, Maj. Gen. Lawrence New. [*November 1985*]

155

156

157a

156 **Bruce braves sharks and fuel oil**

HMS Exeter displays her manoeuvrability to the container ship Hoegh Duke during Gulf patrol duty. During her 36,000 mile deployment, the Type 42 destroyer answered a distress call from a wrecked merchantman in the Indian Ocean. Swimming among sharks in heavy seas near a coral reef, ship's diver LAEM Bruce Marks played a "very, very brave" part in an operation which resulted in the rescue of 14 seamen. He volunteered to examine the damage to the 40,000-ton Lion of Piraeus, stranded on the reef near the Farquhar Islands north of Madagascar. Sharks were not the only danger – heavy seas threatened to dash him against the coral or the ship and at times he was swimming in almost pure fuel oil spilling from the freighter. [*January 1986*]

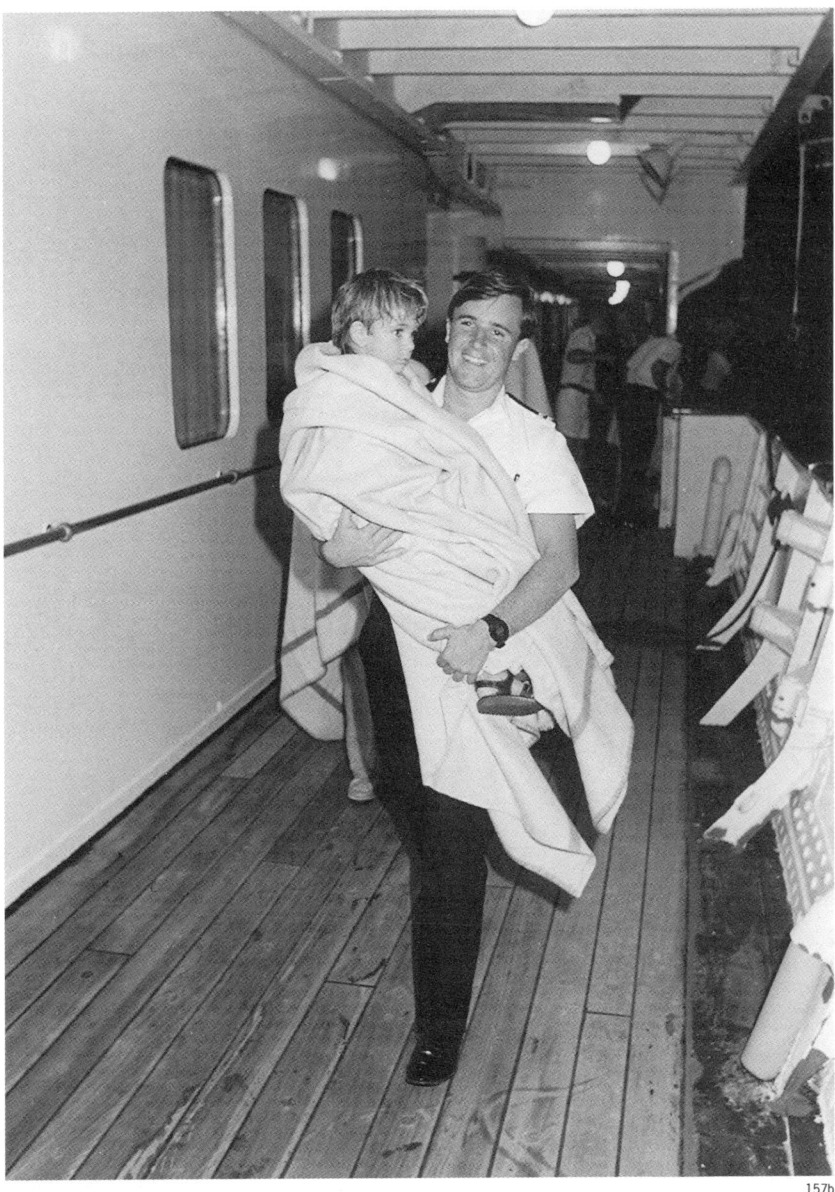

157b

157c

157 **And the band played on**

Tributes for rescuing hundreds of men, women and children from the beaches of war-wracked Aden sent the word world wide that "The Navy's here" spirit flourished as strongly as ever.

In HMY Britannia, which was prominent in the rescue mission, Royal Marines musicians serenaded evacuees as they sailed from the burning city – a morale-boosting eccentricity that seemed to belong to another era but whose message of reassurance was unmistakable.

Proximity of the Royal Yacht – on passage to New Zealand – as the call for help arrived lent the mercy mission special significance. But the Navy's other Indian Ocean patrol ships, HMS Jupiter and HMS Newcastle, the supply ship RFA Brambleleaf and the survey vessel HMS Hydra also became closely involved.

Craft from the Britannia headed for the beaches to ferry some 430 people back to safety. She took them 150 miles across to Djibouti on the East African coast – and then went back to pick up another 209, many of whom were transferred to HMS Jupiter. Later another 40 were taken on board – and by that time she had saved 1,000 people of nearly 50 nations. Mothers with babies and grandmothers were among those who waded out to reach the Britannia's craft while shrapnel flew around beaches eventually engulfed by the fighting.

The Britannia's Royal apartments were widely used to accommodate the refugees who, wrapped in towels and blankets and warmed with soup and "oggies", dossed down on deep pile carpets beneath signed photographs of the Queen Mother.

Yachtsmen took it in turns to babysit while parents bathed and showered and enjoyed their first change of clothing in a week.

British Ambassador Arthur Marshall commented: "What we would have done if the Britannia had not appeared I shudder to think. It would have been a bloodbath of unspeakable proportions."

Kept away from the shore by the 12-mile limit rule, the British warships played an important role in maintaining contact with people on shore – but the special status of the Britannia had allowed her to go in closer than grey-line vessels and gave her a unique wartime evacuation experience which was said to have delighted The Queen. [*February 1986*]

158 **Damage limitation exercise that worked well**

Work was going on around the clock to repair major fire damage which postponed the departure of HMS Illustrious on the world deployment Global 86. The fire occurred in the forward gearing room just hours after the ship had left after a busy maintenance and storing period in Portsmouth Naval Base. The carrier limped back into harbour to receive the attentions of a crowd of Press reporters and cameramen, but such was the speed and efficiency of the fire-fighting operation that the incident was turned into something of a public relations triumph. The graphically proven success of safety techniques introduced in the aftermath of the Falklands War offered immediate reassurance – and a new openness in PR direction helped to put the message across. "Ten years ago we wouldn't even have been allowed through the Dockyard gates," one seasoned reporter commented approvingly.

The Type 22 frigate HMS Beaver assumed the role of flagship for Rear Admiral Robin Hogg and she sailed with other ships of the task group as planned. The Illustrious eventually sailed on July 21 after trials in the Channel to test the renewed gearbox. Working in the restored gearing room on pre-start checks are MEM(M) Shawn McKluskey (left) and MEM(M) Jim Welsh. [*May 1986*]

158a

158b

159

160

159 *Shades of 'On the Beach' for Swiftsure*

With the mist-shrouded Golden Gate Bridge ahead of her, the nuclear powered Fleet submarine HMS Swiftsure makes for a well-earned run ashore in San Francisco – a scene widely reminiscent of Stanley Kubrick's bleak postnuclear holocaust fantasy 'On The Beach' when a lone submarine returned to find the city devoid of life and heavily contaminated by radio-active fall-out. (See page 8)

Despite appearances, the Swiftsure's reception this time was warm and friendly as ever. She had sailed in March to do her bit in the Global 86 deployment, with operations in the North and South Atlantic and Pacific Oceans – including a spell of duty off the Falkland Islands – and San Francisco was her first port of call in 11 weeks.The exercise RIMPAC (Rim of the Pacific) involving vessels from the UK, USA, Australia, Canada and Japan would follow, ending with a call at Pearl Harbour, Hawaii. [*July 1986*]

160 *Close to the edge – Beaver does the samba*

HMS Beaver performs her dance routine off Central America. Although the Global 86 ships were reputed to have been warned by a signal from the Flat Earth Society that they would fall off the edge on April 23, landfall had been safely made off the West Indies... A few days later the group entered the main Venezuelan port of La Guaira and Rear Admiral Hogg went on to Caracas to lay a wreath at the memorial to the country's liberator, Simon Bolivar. Towing her sonar array from the Gulf of Panama to Acapulco, the Beaver entertained orphaned children who had lost their parents in the Mexico City earthquake before moving further north to San Diego. (*July 1986*)

161

161 Swallow tailed by a titan

Hong Kong patrol craft HMS Swallow is dwarfed by the 58,000 ton battleship USS New Jersey as she escorts the 1940s veteran to her mooring. The largest battleship afloat was paying a five-day goodwill visit to the Crown Colony with the destroyer USS Merrill, frigate USS Thatch and supply vessel USS Wabash. [*August 1986*]

162

162 Diana takes a dive

"I've had a whale of a time," the Princess of Wales joked as she returned from her visit to HMS Trafalgar.

Princess Diana had made a private call on the first of the Royal Navy's latest class of nuclear-powered Fleet submarines on exercise in the Firth of Clyde.

As the boat had just returned from a visit to Brest, she was treated to a cold buffet in the Wardroom which included many delicacies brought from France in honour of the occasion.

"Di dives deep" was typical of the headlines that accompanied this picture – with commanding officer Cdr Toby Elliott – taken by a Royal Navy photographer that made the front pages of most of the national Press. [*October 1986*]

163 Swift Sword's terrible storm

Entering Limassol, Cyprus is HMS Intrepid – then the largest RN unit to visit the island for many years. The amphibious assault ship was on passage to Oman to take part in the large-scale Exercise Saif Sareea (Swift Sword) which involved simultaneous landing by landing craft and Sea King assault helicopters.

With several tons of pyrotechnics used as battle simulation, aircraft attacks by RN Sea Harriers, RAF Tornados and Omani Jaguars, naval gunfire support from RN ships and men of 40 Commando storming the beach at Shiya on Oman's north east coast, the effect was spectacular.

After securing the beach head the Marines started a strenuous four day exercise with elements of the Sultan of Oman's land forces.

The intense heat was broken only once – by torrential rain in a 40 minute storm which produced flash floods, with walls of water thundering down the normally parched wadis.

Royal Navy ships involved included HMS Illustrious, Nottingham and Andromeda with RFAs Fort Grange, Orangeleaf and Olmeda.

163b

• *Above:* In landing craft from HMS Intrepid, men of 40 Commando RM wait to storm the beach. [*January 1987*]

163a

164

164 **Caribbean exercise goes like a train**

HMS Southampton negotiates the narrow entrance to San Juan harbour, Puerto Rico. To her port squats the massive, 16th century Spanish fort of El Morro, while in the foreground a trawler lies wrecked on a sandbar.

Often besieged, the fort has only fallen once – to the English in 1598, and then it had to be taken from behind. Three years before its guns beat off Sir Francis Drake. Still, if 'El Draque' had had the use of HMS Ark Royal – at this time accompanying the Southampton in Exercise Caribtrain – with her squadron of Sea Harriers, the outcome would have been much different. 801 Naval Air Squadron fliers had shown their mettle against the neighbouring US weapons ranges at Vieques – producing, it was said, the most spectacular run of successes ever witnessed there.

Four aircraft flying two separate attacks dropped 1,000 lb bombs to wipe out a SAM missile installation and put an airfield out of action "for no loss". It was rare for them to get the chance to deliver bombs against a proper "hard target" so they made the most of it by dropping 60 over three days – more than the squadron delivered in the whole of the Falklands War.

But a four–day anti-submarine duel with the US Navy had been the real highlight of Caribtrain – the accuracy of the Sea Dart missile system had been proved once again in firings from the Southampton, Ark Royal, Bristol and Liverpool, all of which hit the target. [*April 1987*]

165a

165 **Tragedy at Zeebrugge**

A grim-faced Lieut The Duke of York arrives with his Duchess at Zeebrugge naval base to be met by divers from Portsmouth working on the wreck of the Townsend Thoresen cross-Channel ferry Herald of Free Enterprise.

With Royal Navy and NATO ships in the Zeebrugge area alerted and military transport mobilised from various parts of the UK, one of the first to receive a call was Lieut Steve Wild (here escorting the Duchess of York), staff diving officer to Flag Officer Portsmouth and the man who was to take much of the decision-making responsibility as manager of the UK resources. After 44 hours' work, their sad tally was the recovery of 32 bodies.

CPO Pete Still, leader of the first Portsmouth team to arrive, had 11 years earlier helped remove corpses from the sunken HMS Fittleton.

In the pitch black, he and his colleagues had to struggle through masses of floating debris – cases, trolleys, bottles, broken glass, unused lifejackets and cutlery. Lorries on the vehicle deck were hanging by chains. Visibility in the water was nil.

Below: The wreck of the Herald of Free Enterprise. [*April 1987*]

165b

166a

166b

166 'Gatling guns' for Exeter

HMS Exeter looks spick and span and rarin' to go after a busy period of trials following seven months of changes carried out in Portsmouth Naval Base. Major enhancements to the ship's effectiveness included the fitting of two Phalanx close-in weapon mountings – the super-fast firing Gatling-type gun that, with built-in automatic radar guidance had been seen to offer a highly effective "last ditch" counter to incoming anti-ship missiles. [*June 1987*]

167 **Sea Dart counters stormy Petrel**

Meanwhile what they were calling the Royal Navy's biggest gun – a gleaming 21-inch monster, 29 ft long with a range of 100 miles – was equally impressive in action.

Actually it wasn't a gun at all – Petrel ballistic rocket targets are here being fired from twin portable launchers on the range north of Roosevelt Roads from the flight deck of RFA Olwen.

While HMS Southampton's Sea Dart systems were shown to be up to the mark in countering them, they certainly kept the Ops room staff on their toes.

The big advantage of the Mach 3 Pétrel was that it closely ressembled a variety of air-launched, air-to-surface threats. Developed from a sounding rocket originally produced in the 1950s to launch meteorological and other scientific payloads into the lower reaches of space, the Petrel was seen as a bargain as a target – a much cheaper option at around £1,000 than a radio-controlled drone. [*June 1987*]

167

168 **Peril in the Pentland Firth**

In a dramatic night air-sea rescue HMS Ark Royal helped save the lives of 20 people on board a sinking German trawler in the Pentland Firth.

Two helicopters from 820 Squadron were quickly airborne from the Ark, carrying salvage teams and pumps, after the mayday message was received that the Hessen was in trouble.

When the salvage attempt proved unsuccessful, the trawler crew and RN personnel were lifted off to the carrier – and as the last of them were recovered the vessel capsized and sank, as graphically depicted in this picture flashed to the national Press by the Ark's Photographic Section. [*July 1987*]

168

169

169 Warriors in company

HMS Warrior, Britain's first ironclad now safely "home" at Portsmouth, is seen here soon after the start of her journey south from Hartlepool where she had been faithfully restored to her former glory as the pride of the Fleet in 1861.

Sailing past at one stage of the 400 mile tow was another sleek – but much younger vessel – the Type 21 frigate HMS Arrow. [*August 1987*]

170 A barrel for passing the Barrier

For the first time, the new Type 22 frigate HMS London negotiates the Thames Barrier for her debut in the capital. Top of the list of her engagements during her five-day visit was maintenance of a rarely enacted tradition dating from 14th century, when Richard II decreed that all vessels moored in the Pool of London to the west of the Tower should deliver barrels of wine to the Governor as payment for their safety.

In keeping with that rule, the London's commanding officer, Capt. Robert Fisher – escorted by members of the ship's company and the Head Gaoler of the Tower – marched thither to pay the required dues in the form of a cask of wine. [*September 1987*]

170

171 **Sad eye for Wakeful**

With a tear in her eye – just discernible in this picture – and her ship's company standing with caps doffed, the submarine tender HMS Wakeful was the subject of a sad and solemn ceremony at Faslane.

The wake for the Wakeful was held at the Clyde submarine base before the 90-ton converted tug left for the last time – to pay off for disposal at Portsmouth. HMS Wakeful was the only HM ship permanently supporting the submarine squadrons based on the Clyde. She was built as an ocean-going tug in 1965, and commissioned in the Royal Navy in 1974. At first she was used as a fishery protection vessel, but from 1976 became a familiar sight as she went about her business around Faslane. [*November 1987*]

171a

171b

172

172 **White out of grey**

Fresh out of refit and resplendent in her "new" survey livery after five years' service in the grey Navy on South Atlantic duty, HMS Herald heads through wintry waters off Portland during sea training. [*January 1988*]

173 **Rising above it**

HMS Manchester's lean bows rise clear of the waves in this study of the Type 42 destroyer battling through heavy seas. Photographer – LA(Phot) Chris North. [*February 1988*]

173

174 **All eyes on the Argus**

Trials of the new Royal Fleet Auxiliary air training vessel Argus were under way in the Portsmouth area. Although she had been designed principally as a helicopter training ship, the former container carrier mv Contender Bezant – bought and converted at Belfast at a cost of £65m – had many possibilities. At 28,000 tons, she was bigger than any aircraft carrier in service in the Royal Navy and possessed "probably the only bomb-proof flight deck in the business". The ship's original hangars had been turned upside down and filled with a five-foot layer of concrete before being replaced and having the flight deck welded on top. This had provided the ship with extra stability and enabled a seven-tier accommodation block to be built.

The five-spot flight deck incorporated a structure intended to represent the back of a frigate, so providing the fullest possible training experience for air crews. Up to six helicopters could be accommodated at a time.

In addition to her training function, the Argus could replenish warships with fuel at sea, again increasing the flexibility of her role. During the Gulf War of 1991 she was quickly and easily adapted to double as a hospital ship. [*April 1988*]

174

175

175 **Tenement with a tennis court**

RFA Diligence (left, bows top out of picture) carries out a reverse replenishment at sea from the tanker RFA Tidespring.

Diligence may not have been a pretty sight – one of the more curiously wrought ships serving the Fleet, she had the appearance of a floating tenement surmounted by a tennis court...

But symmetry sank to the bottom of the list of priorities when it came to oiling the works which kept a force of warships running smoothly and effectively far from home.

The Diligence's "tenement" – her high superstructure – is set far forward to leave a clear working area on her upper deck midships and aft. The "tennis court" perched atop is a generous and easily accessible flight deck.

At this time she represented the long arm of forward support in the Gulf where she provided the nuts and bolts for the Cimnel Group – the Navy's mine countermeasures force in the area – as well as providing aid to the destroyers and frigates of the Armilla Patrol. [*July 1988*]

177

176 **A gift to Australia**

As HMS Edinburgh looks on at the Bicentennial Naval Salute in Sydney, HMAS Cook, with the Duke of York embarked, moves between HNLMS Zuiderkruis (left) and RFA Orangeleaf, taking the salute from both ships' companies in turn.

She is followed by her escort HMAS Wollongong and the Sail Training Craft Young Endeavour, a bicentennial gift from the UK to the people of Australia. [*November 1988*]

177 **School photograph**

"Bow Chasers" is still one of the most sought-after photographs published in Navy News. It continues to intrigue, particularly as the Navy was not at the time prepared to identify the submarine by country or class. In fact it shows a school of dolphins riding the bow wave of an Algerian Russian-built boat at dusk in the Mediterranean, photographed by LA(Phot) Chris North then serving at HMS Rooke, who won second prize in the black and white section of the Peregrine Trophy photographic competition. [*January 1989*]

178

178 Last flights from Engadine

After 48,000 deck landings RFA Engadine completed her last voyage in her operational role as the Royal Navy's aviation training ship.

It was back in the early 60s, with the advent of destroyers and frigates designed to operate their own helicopter flights, that the demand for rotary-wing-trained aircrew surged. So, too, did the need for maintenance personnel with experience of working at sea.

It would have disrupted programmes too severely to give operational training to new crews on board existing aircraft carriers, so in 1964 an order was placed with Henry Robb's yard at Leith for a helicopter support ship.

With two Avcat fuel tanks below decks, the Engadine had sufficient fuel to allow her embarked helicopters between two and three weeks' flying. Operating out of Portland, she spent between 60 and 70 per cent of her available time at sea. Her role in "Bomb Alley" as helicopter repair and maintenance vessel during the Falklands War earned her a battle honour.

Here a formation of two Sea Kings from 810 Naval Air Squadron Culdrose and two Lynx from 702 NAS Portland fly over RFA Engadine in Falmouth Bay as she left to complete her final few days as aviation training ship before handing over to RFA Argus. [*April 1989*]

179

179 **Cargo of poison**

Using her manned mini-sub and two more submersibles, the seabed operations vessel HMS Challenger swung her high-tech equipment into action to raise 28 drums of toxic chemicals from the bed of the English Channel.

The Panamanian-registered Perintis, carrying a lethal cargo, went down 35 miles south east of Brixham. Using her computerised plotting system and sonars, the Challenger relocated her within a few hours of arriving in area. She took up dynamic hover over the wreck, manoeuvring in delicate one-metre steps until the remote-operated vessels Sprint and Scorpio and the manned submersible LR5 – all fitted with an array of cameras, video recorders, sonars, echo sounders, manipulator arms, cutters and claws – were able to go into action in an operation described by the Challenger's CO, Capt. Mark Masterman, as "a cross between driving through Steptoe's backyard and a china shop".

Eventually its success surpassed all expectations, with 28 of 32 50 kg drums recovered. [*May 1989*]

180 **Harpooning off the Hebrides**

Off the Outer Hebrides the new Type 22 frigate HMS Cumberland fires a Harpoon surface-to-surface missile – the second by a RN warship. The first was from HMS Cornwall the previous autumn, and the firing from the Cumberland formed part of a series of Director General Surface Weapons project firings in support of Fleet weapons acceptance. The commissioning ceremony of the Cumberland took place later at Devonport. [*July 1989*]

180

181 **Victory at sea?**

"Dogged by labour problems, handicapped by the mysterious loss of original plans, the longest refit in the history of the Royal Navy is now 25 years old – and still only three-quarters complete..."

Thus Navy News opened No 405 in its Ships of the Royal Navy series, paying tribute to HMS Victory, the Senior Service's oldest commissioned ship.

Taking no account at all of the declining spending power of Sterling over more than two centuries, it was true to say that the refit bill was already several hundred times the cost of build.

Yet it was undeniably true, too, that the old wooden walls had often provided excellent value for money. On 30 November 1758 all the Royal Navy's First Rates were condemned as unfit for service – but then, the Royal Sovereign had just passed her 121st birthday...

One of 12 "battleships" then ordered to make up the deficiency, HMS Victory was the sole First Rate of the batch. But she proved so useful that varieties of the class continued in build until 1825.

The Victory's active service career ended with the Baltic campaign of 1810-12. Her association with Nelson and Trafalgar saved her from the breaker's yard – but in 1903 the cruiser HMS Neptune accidentally rammed her in Portsmouth Harbour, highlighting the fact that her timbers were by then so rotten that she might easily have foundered of her own accord. The Society for Nautical Research launched an appeal to restore her and she was taken to Portsmouth's historic No 2 Dock, where she now has a permanent home, to begin her fifth major refit, completed in 1927.

Earlier refits had changed her appearance considerably, and the current plan is to recover her state at the time of her finest hour on October 21, 1805. Some 12-14 per cent of her original timbers and a further 30-40 per cent dating from the time of Trafalgar remain – the rotten oak is being replaced with teak and iroko.

Despite the introduction of admission charges, HMS Victory remains one of Britain's most popular historic tourist attractions, her list of visitors rivalling those of many of the country's stately homes.

The publication in Navy News of this "very rare" photograph of HMS Victory under sail produced a huge postbag. Admiral of the Fleet Sir Michael Pollock was one who enjoyed the joke – "especially since I have already caught out several people who ought to have known better."

The remarkably convincing photograph by Wright and Logan – the well known Portsmouth photographers firm whose archive still attracts a world-wide clientele of collectors – showed a quarter-scale sea-going model built at the old Gunboat Yard, Haslar, Gosport in 1931-32.

"As a Midshipman in the Nelson, Home Fleet flagship in 1935-36, I had the great pleasure of sailing in her at and around the 1935 Review of the Fleets at Spithead," wrote Admiral Pollock.

"She was built on the hull of a 54 ft launch – the standard liberty boats for battleships at that time. Sails and rigging were correct in every detail, and a sailing manual for working them (of which I still have a copy) was issued to us for our work up at Portland. The sails were furled and reefed from aloft. I was the foretopman, the only one, because I was small and light and so did not put the light upper yards at risk. She sailed very well – but always had either a picket boat or the Nelson's drifter in attendance in case of calm or imminent disaster in the fast tides of Portland or Solent." [*August 1989*]

181

182 **A bad run ashore?**

As she leaves San Francisco after a five-day visit, HMS Gloucester passes the infamous prison island of Alcatraz. The Type 42 destroyer had earlier handed over West Indies guardship duties to HMS York before visiting Belize City and heading for Acapulco and Long Beach via the Panama Canal. [*September 1989*]

182

The 1990s

Navy News

MARCH 1991 20p

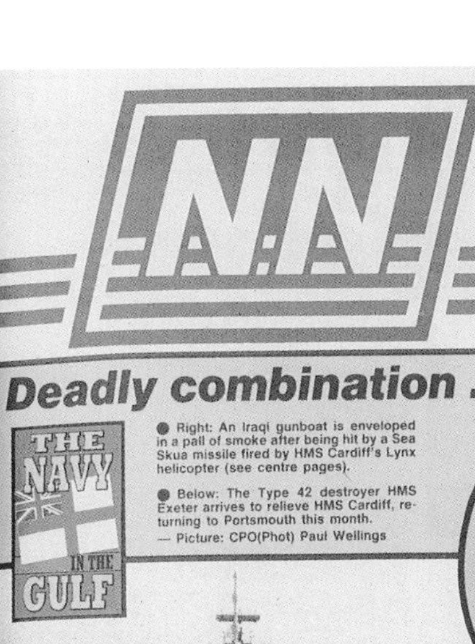

Deadly combination . . . . . . that devastated Saddam at sea

THE NAVY IN THE GULF

● Right: An Iraqi gunboat is enveloped in a pall of smoke after being hit by a Sea Skua missile fired by HMS Cardiff's Lynx helicopter (see centre pages).

● Below: The Type 42 destroyer HMS Exeter arrives to relieve HMS Cardiff, returning to Portsmouth this month.
— Picture: CPO(Phot) Paul Wellings

A quarter of the Iraqi Fleet's losses have been chalked up by the Royal Navy — a fact underlined by Lieut. General Sir Peter de la Billiere, Commanding Officer of British Forces in the Gulf, when he spent two hours on board the Task Group flagship, HMS London.

"When you bear in mind that you're substantially less than 25 per cent of the total of Allied ships at sea in this theatre, that is a very creditable performance," he said.

"We have annihilated Saddam Hussein's ability to produce any opposition at sea."

As he spoke, the total enemy losses were:

- Frigates — one, out of action at Khor Az Zubayr
- Missile patrol boats — six sunk, five damaged
- Major patrol craft — three sunk, two damaged
- Minor patrol craft — 30 sunk, 22 damaged
- Landing craft — three sunk, four damaged
- Major mine warfare vessels — two sunk, one damaged

IRAQI NAVY WIPED OUT

OVER 40 Iraqi vessels have now been destroyed by the Allies — with a hefty share falling to Royal Navy helicopter pilots.

Naval supremacy was claimed within a fortnight of the start of the campaign at sea, the combination of Lynx helicopter and Sea Skua missile proving particularly devastating against enemy surface units (see centre pages).

Recently modified to improve its endurance in action, the Lynx now carries infra-red jammers which send out high-energy beams to deflect incoming heat-seeking missiles.

Commodore Chris Craig, the RN Task Group commander, has described it as "the perfect weapon system for this arena."

Most of the enemy fleet is now sunk or damaged — and the few units remaining are vulnerable whenever they come out of port. The helicopters depredations have not been entirely unopposed, however. HMS Brazen's flight came under fire when on a "search and destroy" mission off the Kuwaiti coast.

"I saw three of four bursts sending plumes of water into the air," Lieut.-Cdr Mike Pearey told Navy News "Over the noise of the helicopter we couldn't hear anything and it was only when I saw the splashes that I realised someone was shooting at us.

"They were a couple of hundred yards short of us and I looked up and I could see the traces of fire coming from the shore. Jon" (his pilot, Lieut. Jon Reid) "remained very cool and banked away sharply, taking us out of the firing line."

HMS Cardiff — whose own Lynx has been pre-eminent in the naval cam-

● Turn to back page

JACK-POT!

For the first time, the Royal Navy is to have a Service lottery, with tickets at 75p a week offering the chance to win a series of prizes based on soccer or cricket results.

While the six prizes each week — top one £2,000 — will bring added flavour to naval life, main object is to boost the hard-pressed funds for sport and recreation in the Service by, hopefully, well over half a million pounds a year.

Finally approved after three years of negotiation, the scheme is due to start in September and initially about 25,000 tickets will be available.

It will be based on FA League matches in winter and County Cricket matches in summer. Those joining (minimum period three months) will receive a card providing a list of

● Turn to page 37

Diana at Drake

FIVE-year-old Carrie Gould, daughter of LS Ken Gould, of HMS Brazen, shyly presents a bouquet to the Princess of Wales who, with the Prince, met Gulf Service families at Drake — see page 29 for more pictures and a special message from the Princess.
Picture: LA(Phot) G.J. Meggitt

12 PER CENT — AND MORE

THIS year's Services pay award brings an average increase for personnel on main scales of just over 12 per cent.

But for the Royal Navy there is a series of "extras", including improvements in the Longer Service at Sea Bonus, a boost in submarine pay, bonuses for young officers on full career commissions, and Separation Allowance improvements.

For full details, including the new daily rates, see page 15. For the Pay Review Body's comments on married quarters and furniture charges, see page 17.

183 **Arrow helps crack the drugs trade**

West Indies guardship HMS Arrow was putting in time to tackle the evil trade of the Colombian drug barons during two patrols with the United States Coast Guard.

Active co-operation by the Royal Navy was and is a barometer of the Government's determination to help in the interception of cocaine and other drugs being smuggled across the Caribbean to Florida. During her first tour with the US Coast Guard the Type 21 frigate helped in the capture of the Beverly Anne - laden with 14,000lb of marijuana.

The Arrow's Lynx helicopter was a vital weapon, extending the search beyond the range of her operations room radar.

Here she links up with the Coast Guard cutter Chincoteague at the start of a week-long patrol. *[February 1990]*

184 **Point of departure**

Seven RN warships and three RFA vessels sail together from Gibraltar for different parts of the globe. The Dartmouth Training Squadron, consisting of HM Ships Bristol, Ariadne and Minerva and RFA Fort Austin, were off on the round-the-world deployment Endeavour 90.

Another four, HMS Cardiff, Charybdis and Liverpool and RFA Bayleaf, were heading for Gulf patrol tasks.

HMS Ambuscade was on her way to South Atlantic duty. *[March 1990]*

183

184

185

185 Homage to Gallipoli

HMS Broadsword off the Golden Horn at Istanbul to mark the 75th anniversary of the Gallipoli campaign of World War I. Veterans from both sides gathered in Turkey for ceremonies attended by Prime Minister Margaret Thatcher, Australian Premier Bob Hawke and Winston Churchill, MP, whose grandfather was the principal architect of the ill-fated plan to drive a wedge between Turkish and German forces and break away from the stalemate of the Western Front in 1915.

In the Dardanelles Straits, through which the Royal Navy had tried to force a passage to Constantinople – the present day Istanbul – HMS Argonaut located the graves of HMS Ocean and HMS Irresistible sunk by shore batteries on 18 March, 1915. Flag Officer Second Flotilla, Rear Admiral Peter Abbott, laid a wreath.

Meanwhile the Broadsword joined in the international sail-past at the Turkish Canakkale war memorial – within sight of the legendary shores of Troy. *[June 1990]*

186

186 Red Indians honour Brave

Fresh from an exhilarating bite at the Big Apple, the carrier HMS Ark Royal leaves New York for Florida as HM ships Cumberland, Brave and Glasgow set off for Canada – the Brave heading to keep an important date with the Six Nations of the Iroquois indians at Hamilton, who had adopted the Type 22 frigate and were preparing to present her commanding officer, Captain Bob Williams, with the eagle feather. This is the sign of peace which is the greatest honour a Red Indian chief can bestow upon a fellow warrior and is not normally presented outside the tribe. *[July 1990]*

The Gulf War

187a

187 Supporting cast for gathering Desert Storm

Soon after the Iraqi invasion of Kuwait eleven Royal Navy and Royal Fleet Auxiliary ships were committed to Gulf and Eastern Mediterranean duty.

The Armilla Patrol vessels HM ships York, Battleaxe and Jupiter were already serving in the Gulf area, Battleaxe having been called from a visit to Penang, Malaysia and Jupiter from a leave period in Mombasa.

Meanwhile three Hunt class vessels, HM ships Cattistock, Hurworth and Atherstone sailed from Rosyth, initially to serve in the Eastern Mediterranean. Leaving Plymouth to act as their support ship was the ocean survey ship HMS Herald. Featuring strongly in the build-up were Royal Fleet Auxiliary vessels. Already RFA Orangeleaf was serving in support of the Armilla ships and more were heading east. The tanker RFA Olna sailed from Devonport with two Sea King Mark 5s embarked and the fleet replenishment vessel RFA Fort Grange left shortly after carrying a pair of Mark 4s. The forward repair ship RFA Diligence, which had been operating away from the UK, was also deployed.

Some of the men who sailed in the Jupiter when she departed Mombasa left behind wives, children and girlfriends who had flown out to be with them during leave.

Working alongside the guided missile cruiser USS England (foreground) in the central area of the Gulf are the Type 22 frigate HMS Batteleaxe (left) and the Leander class frigate HMS Jupiter. [*September 1990*]

ABs Fez Parker and Wiggy Bennett go through upper deck drills in Battleaxe. [*September 1990*]

187b

188

188 **Seven stand together**

Flagship of seven NATO ships, HMS Campbeltown leads the Standing Naval Force Atlantic into Plymouth for a three-and-a-half week maintenance period.

Besides the Devonport-based Type 22 frigate, the flotilla comprised the Gatineau (Canada), Van Kinsbergen (Netherlands), King (USA), Narvik (Norway), Augsburg (Germany) and Sacadura Cabral (Portugal).

Command of the multi-national force rotates between nations. At this time it was held by the Royal Navy's Commodore Mike Gretton. After the Plymouth visit STANAVFORLANT was heading for the USA. [*November 1990*]

189a

189b

189 **War leaders in London**

Senior Naval Officer Middle East Cdre Chris Craig takes Prime Minister John Major to the bridge of HMS London to review the Royal Navy Task Group in the Gulf.

• The London is here in the foreground with HMS Herald leading the main group. [*February 1991*]

190

190 **Saddam's spite**

Against the background of a fierce oilfield blaze an 846 Sqn Sea King embarked in RFA Argus carries out a survey of the coastal area near Kuwait City as part of the Allied clean-up effort in the wake of the Gulf War. Dense clouds of smoke were rising over hundreds of burning oil wells as, vengeful to the last, Saddam Hussein spread a miasma of pollution and a legacy of ruin for his "Arab brethren" to ponder for years to come. [*April 1991*]

191 **Southampton returns to the fold**

HMS Southampton leaves Swan Hunter's Hebburn yard for trials after a major refit and repair package. The Type 42 destroyer had been extensively damaged in a Middle East collision in 1988 and returned "piggy back" to Portsmouth on a heavy lift vessel before being taken on to the Tyne for work which included repairs to hull and superstructure. [*June 1991*]

191

192 **Booby prize for Brocklesby and Co**

The Gulf War was over before minehunters HMS Brocklesby, Brecon and Bicester arrived – but there was still plenty of work for them to do. By this time over half the estimated 1,500 mines sown by the Iraqis had been accounted for – either the tethered contact variety similar to those used in both world wars or the modern type laid on the sea bed and set off by a passing ship's sound signature. They were smeared with organic material to attract fish and mask their presence from the searchers above. The minehunters' submersibles were used to investigate likely contacts – an expensive precaution, as when one of the Brocklesby's accidentally collided with its quarry. Cdre Chris Craig said Navy divers had spent "two dirty, dangerous months" clearing the major ports of Shuaiba, Shuweikh and Kuwait City – "battling through simply atrocious conditions, diving among oil, booby traps and literally hundreds of bodies that had been just dumped off the quayside by the invaders." *[June 1991]*

192

193 **Bringing relief to Bangladesh**

In drenching humidity Royal Marines prepare for a mercy mission through poorly charted waters in cyclone-stricken Bangladesh. Operation Manna was code name for Britain's relief effort, centred on Cox's Bazaar area, where the low lying islands were worst hit. More than a million people needed aid and in one district alone 51,000 had died. The RFA Fort Grange's four Sea King helicopters and six Rigid Raiders managed to deliver 400 tons of stores in a fortnight. *[July 1991]*

193

194

194 **Holding up**

HMS Upholder, the first conventional submarine to be built for the Royal Navy since the last of the Oberon Class, HMS Onyx, in 1966, had completed her safety work up and a set of sonar trials and was fresh from a summer break in the Mediterranean.

She represented a quantum jump in capability over the trusty Oberons particularly in her snort transit – underwater speed endurance and in silence of operation – cost half as much to build as a nuclear boat, much less to maintain and required less than half the crew. Teething troubles with her torpedo tubes were shrugged aside by her commanding officer, Lieut.-Cdr Ian Stallion: "The early Oberons had problems beside which ours pale into insignificance – and they had outstanding careers with half a dozen other navies besides our own." [*September 1991*]

195

195 **New spirit of Endurance in a proud tradition**

Despite the decision to decommission the ice patrol ship HMS Endurance, a Royal Navy presence was to be maintained in the Antarctic by the chartered Norwegian vessel Polar Circle – later to take the Falklands veteran's name in full time service. Wearing the White Ensign and carrying a Royal Navy crew, the 5,000 ton ice-breaker seen here entering Portsmouth Harbour would carry on the longstanding tradition of support for the British Antarctic Survey and carry out hydrographic and meteorological work. [*November 1991*]

"Is it all right with your studio if we open fire?"

Charles Miles summed up the frustrations of the long build-up to the Gulf War while diplomatic pressure tried in vain to force Saddam Hussein to withdraw from Kuwait and RN forces concentrated as the chief support of the US Battle Fleet under a barrage of advice from the media as to how the situation might be resolved.

Index of ships